BLACKSTONE

=OUTDOOR=

GAS GRIDDLE

COOKBOOK

300 Delicious and Easy Grill Recipes, plus Pro Tips & Illustrated
Instructions to Quick-Start with Your Blackstone Outdoor Gas Griddle

Jaime J. Wike

Table of Content

Chapter 4 Pork 44

Chapter 5 Beef and Lamb . 52

Introduction

Traditional versions of griddles involve the use of stones and brick slabs as flat surfaces placed above the fire to heat up to cooking temperature. The resulting heated flat surface is then removed, and food is placed on the surface to cook. As you can see, the historical griddle-cooking method was stressful and left room for several modifications and evolution. In the early 2000s, the Blackstone company sought a cooking appliance that was capable of performing the functions of a regular indoor cooking appliance along with the ability to barbecue like a grill. By 2005, they were able to manufacture their cornerstone product, the 36" Blackstone Griddle that kickstarted the company's long chain of griddle-cooking products.

I had always thought my former gas cooker was jinxed because it had the knack of disappointing me when I needed it most, from the difficulty with getting it to come on to burning my meals to a crisp.

I think what finally broke my heart was the incident on an unforgettable weekend. I already cut the vegetables, with the carrot and onions sliced to my taste, with fresh tomatoes and peppers

that I got from a last-minute trip to the mall.

Everything was set for the special treat I wanted to give my husband and son on a chilly Friday evening. We hadn't had time to get together recently because of their busy schedules, and I desperately needed family time.

I tried turning on the Cooker, but it didn't start even after 2 hours. Its faulty temperature regulation was another hassle I anticipated. Needless to say, the day was a disaster, and we finally had to get some tacos to eat.

I knew it was time for a change, so I turned to Amazon for answers to this particular problem.

I just needed a pleasant cooking experience that won't leave me pulling my hair afterwards or throwing food away because the Cooker burnt it again.

What can I do to make my cooking easier? How can I possibly grill with less stress and at ease, without having itchy eyes?

These were the questions that bothered me a month and two weeks ago before I discovered the Blackstone Outdoor Gas Griddle. Guess what? My cooking has never been any better.

Constituents of Blackstone Outdoor Gas Griddle

The griddle is designed to be easy to operate. The Blackstone Company manufactured many accessories to accompany the griddle, but here are a few basic components present when a Blackstone griddle is purchased.

Griddle Top: This is the main component of the Blackstone griddle; it is where the cooking takes place. It is made of steel and designed as a slope to prevent disturbances from juices while cooking. The griddle top is placed over multiple burners and heated up to the selected cooking temperature.

Side Shelf: This is fixed to the side of the griddle. It can hold seasonings and other ingredients of the food to be prepared. However, do not put heavy materials on the shelf.

Portable Legs: The griddle comes with foldable legs and wheels to allow for easy movement. The caster wheels will have the grill positioned precisely where you want, and it has a lock mechanism to prevent any unwanted movement.

Griddle Drip Dish: This pan is responsible for collecting the juices produced while cooking. The griddle top is positioned at an angle that allows the liquid present on the surface to drip down to the drip pan through a mini steel channel. Removable

Drip Tray: It is present at the bottom of the grill and positioned between the four portable legs. It helps to collect juice when present in excessive amounts.

Control Valves: This controls the direction of all the cooking done on the griddle. The valves are used to set the cooking temperature of the burner Ignition Switch: This button makes igniting the Blackstone griddle easy. It is battery powered and automatic. Once you press the button, the griddle comes alive and starts to heat up to the temperature selected with the control valve.

Since discovering the Blackstone Outdoor Gas Griddle, I have never had a reason to miss my old Cooker because this upgrade has made a remarkable difference in my overall grilling experience with its outstanding and efficient features. In front of the Blackstone gas griddle, I feel like Myron Mixon, who is currently the best BBQ chef in the world.

This gas griddle is very simple to use and easy to operate; you'll be grilling better in no time. It has continually helped me prepare the tastiest grilled veggies and proteins, which has been a lifesaver when I have friends and family over.

The Blackstone Outdoor Gas Griddle comes with a four-wheel easy to push handle that allows you to take it outside when you feel like getting fresh air or for barbecue nights. It also features an easy to start push button, with just a click, your Gas Griddle will help you make that tasty mouthwatering dish that will have you and your guests drooling.

I have had a big pile of different recipes that I bought months ago but haven't been able to try out because I didn't even know how to begin. My hesitation to explore these new recipes was due to my messy old Cooker and my overactive imagination of all that could go wrong. But with the Blackstone Outdoor Gas Griddle I got, I could make perfect use of it. Would you believe it if I said I had tried almost all of them out, within a space of four weeks that I got the Blackstone Outdoor Gas Griddle

Tools and Trade

First, you're going to need the right tools to cook on and maintain your new griddle top. Make sure to purchase two spatulas because you'll be using both hands like the chefs at Japanese steakhouses before you're done! It's also a good idea to have two spatulas so you can avoid cross-contaminating different foods. There are many different types of spatulas on the market. Many have slots in the spatula which allow oils and grease to pass through the spatulas.You'll also want to pick up a good griddle scraper and/or chopper. The scraper is the most essential tool you'll

need for your new griddle. Before long, scraping your griddle top will become as natural as seasoning it. Scrape off particles prior to cooking and scrape off food residue when you're finished cooking. I personally like a designated scraper with a somewhat sharp scraping end. Scraper/chopper tools allow you to chop & dice up vegetables on the griddle while you're cooking. I also frequently use metal tongs to do everything from flip steaks to roll sausages. Lastly, make sure to pick up a few squeezable oil bottles. You can keep your go-to oils in the bottles. They're fairly small and easy to pick up when you're in the midst of cooking on the griddle. I always have a bottle with vegetable or canola oil along with another bottle that's filled with olive oil on hand. If you plan on cooking plenty of Asian-inspired dishes, you can have a bottle of sesameoil handy. If the griddle looks dry, give it a squirt of oil. You get the point

Quite Portable

It comes with four wheels that make it very balanced and allows you to push it to any corner. This effortless mobility makes it easy to carry and move about either to the backyard or front yard.

A Unique Upgrade

My experience with Blackstone showed me the difference between a standard cooking gas and any other cooking instrument. You no longer have to deal with substandard cookers and annoying gas fumes that leave you frustrated and makes the cooking experience less enjoyable.

This Blackstone Outdoor Gas Griddle makes your life easier, your cooking faster, and gives you a whole new experience that improves your cooking skills. Now when people ask me about my hobby, I proudly tell them grilling is top of the list.

Different Heat Zones

The gas griddle has up to 4 heat zones on its surface that can be adjusted to suit your taste. It means you can cook four different food items at the same time or you can be cooking on one side and warm your already cooked food on the other side of the stove.

Trust me; you won't burn a thing! It's especially perfect for house parties or other parties where you have to cook dishes simultaneously. You can have your steaks grilling at a higher temperature than your burger buns or veggies.

Barbecues

The Blackstone Outdoor Gas Griddle is perfect for barbecues and other cookouts that involve an expanded and elaborate cooking surface. My barbecue steak and vegetables always turn out so perfectly grilled; you can't help yourself (I had to break my dietary plans once to get a taste of the barbecue).

Last Tuesday, Junior came back from school hungry and resigned to eating his usual Pizza that I am obliged to get for him when I'm late cooking. Imagine the look on my sons face when he saw the beautifully plated Teriyaki chicken and veggie skewers fresh off the grill. I think he still can't believe it till now.

Now, the Pizza has been cut out of the family menu until further notice. All thanks to the Blackstone outdoor gas griddle my family all eating healthy now.

Expanded Cooktop

When it comes to cooking for an individual, perhaps you, your hubby, and your kid, Blackstone is the only option. When hosting a party, or a get-together, or any event that involves bringing many people around, Blackstone also has you covered. It's four cooking tops allows you to cook different meals at the same time.

Imagine having many guests over and waiting for your alluring brisket. There is no time to grill one after another; the Blackstone outdoor grill allows you BBQ multiple cuts at once.

Whether you are toasting burger buns, grilling a bunch of crunchy veggies, or searing a steak to attain that perfect medium-rare, Blackstone gas griddle is the ideal option for you. What better way for you to multitask and save time, than grilling different items simultaneously.

How It Works

The mechanism of operation of the Blackstone Griddle is similar to the process of traditional griddle-cooking. They both involve the heating of a flat surface, which eventually performs the cooking. But with the Blackstone Griddle, there is no need to remove the cooking surface from direct heat because it has control valves that regulate the temperature. The Blackstone Griddle uses propane or butane LPG bottle gas as a fuel source for creating controlled fire. When the griddle is set to a particular temperature with the control valves and switched on with the ignition switch, the inbuilt igniter needles create a fire in the burner tube. The burner tube is positioned below the griddle top and is responsible for heating it to the desired temperature.

Unlike the traditional griddle-cooking, food is prepared directly on the heated Blackstone Griddle Top. The heat generated allows the griddle to fry, grill, and sear. Here is a step-by-step direction for igniting the Blackstone Griddle:

1. Check the battery of the ignition switch to ensure it is correctly installed.

2. Release the gas with the control valve on the gas bottle and at the cylinder.

3. Turn the control valves on the griddle until the indicator line points to high.

4. Press the ignition switch quickly. You should hear a click and Preheat the griddle for 3-5 minutes before cooking every meal.

Preparation and Maintenance

Think of your griddle top the same way you think of cast iron cookware. However, your griddle top is made of rolled steel. The more you season it, the better your cooking experience will be. Basically, seasoning is applying oil to the griddle top, spreading it around, wiping off the excess, heating it and allowing it to form a non-stick blackened coating on your cooking surface. Regular cooking will provide much of the necessary seasoning.The Blackstone griddle tops come coated with rust protective oil from the factory. Before you use it the first time, you'll want to wash it with a grease-cutting dish soap and rinse. Coat your griddle top (both top and bottom) with cooking oil prior to its first use. You'll notice a brownish, black color start to appear on your griddle top as you adjust the temperature from low to high. Your griddle top is getting discolored. Don't worry; it's exactly what you want to happen. You're on your way to achieving a perfectly seasoned grill that will help to prevent food from sticking to the steel surface. The seasoning also helps achieve that picture-perfect coating on the outside of your food. Finally, the seasoning prevents rust from building up on your griddle top. When you get into the swing of things, seasoning your griddle top will become second nature. You'll do it before, during, and after each time you cook.

Tips To Use Blackstone Griddle

Operating and cooking with the Blackstone griddle isn't tricky, but here a few tips to make your meals successful:

Season your grill regularly: Unlike synthetically coated griddles and grills, Blackstone's cold-rolled steel needs to be seasoned periodically to become non-stick. Seasoning also protects the surface from rusting. Get some Stainless-Steel Spatulas: While Pan Scrapers are okay, the stainless-steel spatulas are the real deal. Get two spatulas and use them to maneuver, mix, and flip your ingredients while cooking on the grill. The use of two spatulas will help manage your food better and prevent cross-contamination.

Prepare all your ingredients before cooking: The griddle is fast-paced and won't wait for you to start chopping up the ingredients. While trying to prepare the next round of food, you may end up burning the items already on the grill. Like the adage says, "to fail to plan is to plan to fail." Invest in Large trays: These trays are essential to transport and hold all your cooking items; it's easier to keep track of all the ingredients when they are in one spot. Purchase some Wire Racks: They help to keep your food away from direct heat. If the food is ready but you are not yet ready to serve, you can put it on the wire rack to keep it hot but away from the heated surface. To transfer away from the griddle, fit a spatula underneath the wire rack and lift.

Use water while cooking: Water cooks the food faster and gives it flavor. You just need to squeeze a little water on the griddle top, and it will convert to steam that will cook the food. Have different bottles for different ingredients: It's easier to keep track of your juices (ketchup, mayo, water) when they exist individually in appropriately labelled containers. Get an Infrared (IR) Gun and an Instant Read Thermometer: The griddle does not have an internal thermometer that measures heat, so an IR gun can be used for cooking foods that require particular temperatures, such as searing. The Instant Read Thermometer can be used when measuring the internal temperature of meat, such as chicken or pork. With the thermometer, preparing a medium-rare steak becomes easy. Magnetic Paper Towel Holder: Regular paper towels are quite challenging to manage while simultaneously trying to grill. The magnetic holder keeps the towel in place and makes it easier for you to tear while griddling at the same time. Cook A Lot: Due to the delicious food and aroma produced with the Blackstone griddle, ensure you cook more than enough because your neighbors are sure to come knocking.

In conclusion, I have had an enjoyable cooking journey since I found out about the Blackstone Outdoor Gas Griddle. My cooking has been made easy, faster with less stress, and gives me a balanced blend of flavors I want. That was why I decided to write a cookbook based on Blackstone Outdoor Gas Griddle to help enhance your cooking skills and make your cooking experience more enjoyable.

Chapter 1 Breakfast

Classic French Toast

Prep time: 5 minutes | Cook time: 10 minutes | Serves 4

6 eggs, beaten
¼ cup "half and half" or heavy cream
8 slices thick cut white or sourdough bread
2 tablespoons sugar
1 tablespoon cinnamon
1 teaspoon salt butter
Powdered sugar
Maple syrup

1. Heat your griddle to medium heat.
2. In a large bowl, combine the eggs, cream, sugar, cinnamon, and salt. Mix well until smooth.
3. Lightly grease the griddle with butter or vegetable oil.
4. Dip each slice of bread in the mixture until well saturated with egg then place onto the griddle.
5. When the French toast has begun to brown, flip and cook until the other side has browned as well. About four minutes.

Sausage Pancakes

Prep time: 6 minutes | Cook time: 8 minutes | Serves 4

Buttermilk Pancake batter
8 breakfast sausage links

1. Make the buttermilk pancake batter.
2. Bring the griddle grill to medium-high heat.
3. Cook the breakfast sausage links until they are completely cooked through, with the juices running clear, or when they reach an internal temperature of 165ºF (74ºC), then set aside and keep warm.
4. Follow the directions for making buttermilk pancakes. Using your spatula, coax the pancake to roll around the sausage link like a blanket. Allow to continue cooking with the sausage in the middle until the pancake is fully cooked.

Mexican Scramble

Prep time: 5 minutes | Cook time: 10 minutes | Serves 4

8 eggs, beaten
1 pounds (454 g) Chorizo
½ yellow onion
1 cup cooked black beans
½ cup green chilies
½ cup jack cheese
¼ cup green onion, chopped
½ teaspoon black pepper vegetable oil

1. Preheat a griddle to medium heat. Brush the griddle with vegetable oil and add the chorizo to one side and the onions to the other side.
2. When the onion has softened, combine it with the chorizo and add the beans and chilies.
3. Add the eggs, cheese, and green onion and cook until eggs have reached desired firmness.
4. Remove the scramble from the griddle and season with black pepper before serving

Cheesy Ham and Pineapple Sandwich

Prep time: 10 minutes | Cook time: 20 minutes | Serves 4

1 (10-ounce / 283-g) package deli sliced ham
4 pineapple rings
4 slices swiss cheese
8 slices of thick bread
Butter, softened, for brushing

1. Butter one side of all the slices of bread and heat your griddle to medium heat.
2. On top of each piece of bread, stack ¼ of the ham, a pineapple ring, and 1 slice of cheese.
3. Place the sandwiches on the griddle and top with another slice of bread.
4. Cook until the bottom bread is golden brown, then flip and cook until the other side of the bread is browned and the cheese is melted.

Ultimate Breakfast Burrito

Prep time: 5 minutes | Cook time: 20 minutes | Serves 2

4 eggs
4 strips bacon
1 large russet potato, peeled and cut into small cubes
1 red bell pepper
½ yellow onion
1 ripe avocado, sliced
2 tablespoon hot sauce
2 large flour tortillas
Vegetable oil

1. Preheat the griddle to medium-high heat on one side and medium heat on the other side. Brush with vegetable oil and add the bacon to the medium heat side and peppers and onions to the medium-high side.
2. When the bacon finishes cooking, place on paper towels and chop into small pieces. Add the potatoes to the bacon fat on the griddle. Cook the potatoes until softened.
3. Add the eggs to the vegetable side and cook until firm. Place the ingredients onto the tortillas and top with slices of avocado and a tablespoon of hot sauce. Fold the tortillas and enjoy.

Hash Brown Scramble

Prep time: 10 minutes | Cook time: 10 minutes | Serves 4

2 russet potatoes, shredded, rinsed, and drained
8 eggs, beaten
1 cup cheddar cheese
6 slices bacon, cut into small pieces
1/3 cup green onion, chopped
Vegetable oil

1. Preheat griddle to medium heat and brush with vegetable oil.
2. On one side, place the potatoes on the griddle and spread in a ½ inch thick layer. Cook the potatoes until golden brown and then flip. Add the bacon to the other side of the griddle and cook until the fat has rendered.
3. Add the eggs and cheese to the top of the hash browns and stir in the bacon and green onion. Cook until the cheese has melted and divide equally among 4 plates.

Toad In a Hole

Prep time: 10 minutes | Cook time: 5 minutes | Serves 4

4 slices white, wheat, or sourdough bread
4 eggs
2 tablespoons butter
Salt and black pepper, to taste

1. Preheat griddle to medium heat add the butter, spreading it around.
2. Cut a hole in the center of each slice of bread.
3. Place the slices of bread on the griddle and crack an egg into the holes in each slice of bread.
4. Cook until the bread begins to brown, then flip and cook until the egg whites are firm.
5. Remove from the griddle and season with salt and black pepper before serving.

Classic Denver Omelet

Prep time: 5 minutes | Cook time: 10 minutes | Serves 2

6 large eggs
¼ cup country ham, diced
¼ cup yellow onion, finely chopped
¼ cup green bell pepper, chopped
2/3 cup cheddar cheese, shredded
¼ teaspoon cayenne pepper
Salt and black pepper, to taste
2 tablespoons butter

1. Heat your griddle to medium heat and place the butter onto the griddle.
2. Add the ham, onion, and pepper to the butter and cook until the vegetables have just softened.
3. Beat the eggs in a large bowl and add a pinch of salt and the cayenne pepper.
4. Split the vegetables into to portions on the griddle and add half of the eggs to each portion. Cook until the eggs have begun to firm up, and then add the cheese to each omelet.
5. Fold the omelets over and remove from the griddle. Serve immediately.

Simple French Crepes

Prep time: 10 minutes | Cook time: 15 minutes | Serves 4

1¼ cups flour
¾ cup whole milk
½ cup water
2 eggs

3 tablespoons unsalted butter, melted
1 teaspoon vanilla
2 tablespoon sugar

1. In a large bowl, add all the ingredients and mix with a whisk. Make sure the batter is smooth. Rest for 1 hour.
2. Heat your Blackstone Griddle to medium heat and add a thin layer of butter. Add about ¼ cup of the batter. Using a crepe spreading tool, form your crepe and cook for 1-2 minutes. Use your Crepe Spatula and flip. Cook for another minute.
3. Top with Nutella and strawberries for a sweet crepe, or top with scrambled eggs and black forest ham for a savory crepe

Fluffy Blueberry Pancakes

Prep time: 15 minutes | Cook time: 10 minutes | Serves 2

1 cup flour
¾ cup milk
2 tablespoons white vinegar
2 tablespoons sugar
1 teaspoon baking powder
½ teaspoon baking

soda
½ teaspoon salt
1 egg
2 tablespoons butter, melted
1 cup fresh blueberries
Butter for cooking

1. In a bowl, combine the milk and vinegar. Set aside for two minutes.
2. In a large bowl, combine the flour, sugar, baking powder, baking soda, and salt. Stir in the milk, egg, blueberries, and melted butter. Mix until combined but not totally smooth.
3. Heat your griddle to medium heat and add a little butter. Pour the pancakes onto the griddle and cook until one side is golden brown. Flip the pancakes and cook until the other side is golden.
4. Remove the pancakes from the griddle and serve with warm maple syrup

Garlic Parmesan Grilled Cheese Sandwich

Prep time: 5 minutes | Cook time: 7 minutes | Serves 1

2 slices Italian bread, sliced thin
2 slices provolone cheese
2 tablespoons butter, softened

Garlic powder, for dusting
Dried parsley, for dusting
Parmesan Cheese, shredded, for dusting

1. Spread butter evenly across 2 slices of bread and sprinkle each buttered side with garlic and parsley.
2. Sprinkle a few tablespoons of Parmesan cheese over each buttered side of bread and gently press the cheese into the bread.
3. Preheat the griddle to medium heat and place one slice of bread, buttered side down, into the skillet.
4. Top with provolone slices and second slice of bread with the butter side up.
5. Cook 3 minutes, and flip to cook 3 minutes on the other side; cook until bread is golden and parmesan cheese is crispy.
6. Serve warm with your favorite sides

Tangy Chicken Sandwich

Prep time: 10 minutes | Cook time: 20 minutes | Serves 4

2 pounds (907 g) chicken breast, sliced into 4 cutlets
4 potato buns, toasted
For the Marinade:
½ cup pickle juice

1 tablespoon Dijon mustard
1 teaspoon paprika
½ teaspoon black pepper
½ teaspoon salt

1. Mix marinade ingredients together in a mixing bowl.
2. Place chicken in marinade and marinate for 30 minutes in the refrigerator.
3. Preheat griddle to medium-high. Wipe off extra marinade and sear chicken for 7 minutes per side, or until a meat thermometer reaches 165ºF (74ºC).
4. Allow chicken to rest for 5 minutes after grilling and serve on toasted buns.

Ultimate Grilled Cheese

Prep time: 10 minutes | Cook time: 10 minutes | Serves 4

8 slices sourdough bread
4 slices provolone cheese
4 slices yellow American cheese
4 slices sharp cheddar cheese
4 slices tomato
3 tablespoons mayonnaise
3 tablespoons butter

1. Heat your griddle to medium heat.
2. Butter one side of each piece of bread and spread mayo on the other side.
3. Place the buttered side down on the griddle and stack the cheeses on top.
4. Place the other pieces of bread, butter side up on top of the cheese and cook until golden brown. Flip and cook until the other piece of bread is golden brown as well and the cheese is melted.
5. Remove from the griddle, slice in half and enjoy

Bacon Egg and Cheese Sandwich

Prep time: 5 minutes | Cook time: 10 minutes | Serves 4

4 large eggs
8 strips of bacon
4 slices cheddar or American cheese
8 slices sourdough
bread
2 tablespoons butter
2 tablespoons vegetable oil

1. Heat your griddle to medium heat and place the strips of bacon on one side. Cook until just slightly crispy.
2. When the bacon is nearly finished, place the oil on the other side of the griddle and crack with eggs onto the griddle. Cook them either sunny side up or over medium.
3. Butter one side of each slice of bread and place them butter side down on the griddle. Place a slice of cheese on 4 of the slices of bread and when the cheese has just started to melt and the eggs are finished, stack the eggs on the bread.
4. Add the bacon to the sandwiches and place the other slice of bread on top. Serve immediately.

Sausage and Mushroom Scramble

Prep time: 10 minutes | Cook time: 20 minutes | Serves 4

8 eggs, beaten
½ pound (227 g) sausage, sliced into thin rounds or chopped
1 green bell pepper, sliced
1 yellow onion, sliced
1 cup white mushrooms, sliced
1 teaspoon salt
½ teaspoon black pepper
Vegetable oil

1. Preheat the griddle to medium-high heat.
2. Brush the griddle with vegetable oil and add the peppers and mushrooms. Cook until lightly browned and then add the onions. Season with salt and pepper and cook until the onions are soft.
3. Add the sausage to the griddle and mix with the vegetables. Cook until lightly browned.
4. Add the eggs and mix with the vegetables and cook until eggs reach desired doneness. Use a large spatula to remove the scramble from the griddle and serve immediately.

Steak and Eggs

Prep time: 10 minutes | Cook time: 10 minutes | Serves 4

1 pound (454 g) Sirloin, cut into 4 ½-inch thick pieces
8 large eggs
3 tablespoons vegetable oil
Salt and black pepper, to taste

1. Preheat griddle to medium-high heat on one side and medium heat on the other.
2. Season the steaks with a generous amount of salt and pepper.
3. Place steaks on the medium high side and cook for 3 minutes and add the oil to the medium heat side.
4. Flip the steaks and crack the eggs onto the medium heat side of the griddle.
5. After 3 minutes remove the steaks from the griddle and allow to rest 5 minutes. Finish cooking the eggs and place two eggs and one piece of steak on each plate to serve. Season the eggs with a pinch of salt and pepper.

Potato Cheese Hash Brown Scramble

Prep time: 10 minutes | Cook time: 10 minutes | Serves 4

2 russet potatoes, shredded, rinsed, and drained
8 eggs, beaten
1 cup cheddar cheese

6 slices bacon, cut into small pieces
1/3 cup green onion, chopped
Vegetable oil

1. Preheat griddle to medium heat and brush with vegetable oil.
2. On one side, place the potatoes on the griddle and spread in a ½ inch thick layer. Cook the potatoes until golden brown and then flip. Add the bacon to the other side of the griddle and cook until the fat has rendered.
3. Add the eggs and cheese to the top of the hash browns and stir in the bacon and green onion. Cook until the cheese has melted and divide equally among 4 plates.

Potato and Bacon Hash

Prep time: 10 minutes | Cook time: 3 hours | Serves 6 to 8

6 slices thick cut bacon
2 russet potatoes, cut into ½ inch chunks
1 yellow onion, chopped
1 red bell pepper, chopped

1 clove garlic, finely chopped
1 teaspoon salt
½ teaspoon black pepper
1 tablespoon Tabasco sauce

1. Set your griddle to medium heat and cook the bacon until just crispy.
2. Add the potato, onion, and bell pepper to the griddle and cook until the potato has softened. Use the large surface of the griddle to spread out the ingredients.
3. When the potato has softened, add the garlic, salt, and pepper.
4. Chop the bacon into small pieces and add it to the griddle. Stir the mixture well and add the hot sauce right before removing the hash from the griddle. Serve immediately.

Chicken Sandwiches

Prep time: 10 minutes | Cook time: 20 minutes | Serves 4

2 pounds (907 g) chicken breast, sliced into 4 cutlets

4 potato buns, toasted

For the Marinade:
½ cup pickle juice
1 tablespoon dijon mustard
1 teaspoon paprika

½ teaspoon black pepper
½ teaspoon salt

1. Mix marinade ingredients together in a mixing bowl.
2. Place chicken in marinade and marinate for 30 minutes in the refrigerator.
3. Preheat griddle to medium-high. Wipe off extra marinade and sear chicken for 7 minutes per side, or until a meat thermometer reaches 165ºF (74ºC).
4. Allow chicken to rest for 5 minutes after grilling and serve on toasted buns.

Chorizo and Black Beans Scramble

Prep time: 5 minutes | Cook time: 10 minutes | Serves 4

8 eggs, beaten
1 pound (454 g) Chorizo
½ yellow onion
1 cup cooked black beans
½ cup green chilies

½ cup jack cheese
¼ cup green onion, chopped
½ teaspoon black pepper
Vegetable oil

1. Preheat a griddle to medium heat. Brush the griddle with vegetable oil and add the chorizo to one side and the onions to the other side.
2. When the onion has softened, combine it with the chorizo and add the beans and chilies.
3. Add the eggs, cheese, and green onion and cook until eggs have reached desired firmness.
4. Remove the scramble from the griddle and season with black pepper before serving.

Eggs Cheese Belledict with Bacon

Prep time: 5 minutes | Cook time: 7 minutes | Serves 2

1 medium red or green bell pepper
2 English muffins
2 eggs
4 slices Canadian bacon
½ cup very finely shredded Jarlsberg cheese
Butter, as needed

1. Bring the griddle grill to medium heat. Cut the uneven bottom off the bell pepper, then cut two rings of pepper about ½ inch thick.
2. Coat the griddle with a good amount of butter. Separate the English muffins and place the uncut-sides on the griddle to begin warming. Place the bell pepper rings on the griddle and cook for 2 minutes. Flip the peppers, then flip the English muffins to heat the other sides.
3. Crack an egg and carefully drop it into one of the bell pepper rings. Scoot the other pepper ring close by and repeat with the second egg. Using a cover that's just bigger than the peppers, cover the eggs and allow them to cook for 1 minute.
4. While the eggs are cooking, warm the Canadian bacon on the grilling surface.
5. Remove the cover from the eggs and squirt water around the grilling surface very close to the eggs, and immediately cover the eggs again to capture the steam and assist with cooking the whites and yolks. Cook for another minute, then cover each of the eggs with half of the cheese. The finer the cheese is grated, the more quickly it will melt, so I use a very fine grater or even a Microplane. Squirt the perimeter of the eggs again and cover to catch the steam, allowing the cheese to melt.
6. Remove the English muffins from the griddle and put 2 slices of Canadian bacon on top of each. Uncover the eggs, and using a spatula, remove the pepper ring containing the egg and slide it onto the Canadian bacon. Top with the other half of the English muffin.

Sausage and Vegetable Scramble

Prep time: 10 minutes | Cook time: 20 minutes | Serves 4

8 eggs, beaten
½ pound (227 g) sausage, sliced into thin rounds or chopped
1 green bell pepper, sliced
1 yellow onion, sliced
1 cup white mushrooms, sliced
1 teaspoon salt
½ teaspoon black pepper
Vegetable oil

1. Preheat the griddle to medium-high heat.
2. Brush the griddle with vegetable oil and add the peppers and mushrooms. Cook until lightly browned and then add the onions. Season with salt and pepper and cook until the onions are soft.
3. Add the sausage to the griddle and mix with the vegetables. Cook until lightly browned.
4. Add the eggs and mix with the vegetables and cook until eggs reach desired doneness. Use a large spatula to remove the scramble from the griddle and serve immediately.

Ice Cream French Toast

Prep time: 5 minutes | Cook time: 8 minutes | Serves 4

1 cup melted vanilla ice cream
3 eggs
1 teaspoon vanilla extract
Pinch of ground cinnamon
8 slices Texas toast or other thick-cut bread
Cooking oil, as needed

1. Combine the melted ice cream, eggs, vanilla extract, and cinnamon in a bowl wide enough for the bread to be easily dipped into. Mix very well or until frothy.
2. Bring the griddle grill to medium-high heat and coat the surface with oil. When the oil begins to shimmer, dip each side of the bread into the egg batter so it lightly coats each side. Allow any additional batter to drain back into the bowl.
3. Place the bread on the griddle. Cook for 3 to 4 minutes per side, or until the French toast is golden brown. Repeat with the remaining ingredients.

Buttermilk Pancakes

Prep time: 5 minutes | Cook time: 6 minutes | Serves 2 to 4

2 cups all-purpose flour	soda
3 tablespoons sugar	Pinch kosher salt
2 teaspoons baking powder	2 eggs
2 teaspoons baking	2½ cups buttermilk
	¼ cup melted butter

1. Sift the flour, sugar, baking powder, baking soda, and salt together in a large bowl.
2. In a medium bowl, whisk the eggs, buttermilk, and melted butter together until frothy, then pour into the dry ingredients. Mix until well combined but do not over mix. Small lumps will be fine. Let sit at room temperature for 20 to 30 minutes while your grill heats up.
3. Bring the griddle grill to medium-high heat. Oil the griddle and allow it to heat until the oil is shimmering but not smoking.
4. Pour about ¼ cup batter onto the griddle grill for each pancake. The pancakes should slowly begin to form bubbles. After 2 to 4 minutes, when the bubbles pop and leave small holes, flip the pancake. Cook for an additional 2 minutes.

Bacon and Gruyere Omelet

Prep time: 5 minutes | Cook time: 15 minutes | Serves 2

6 eggs, beaten	per
6 strips bacon	1 teaspoon salt
¼ pound (113 g) gruyere, shredded	1 tablespoon chives, finely chopped
1 teaspoon black pep-	Vegetable oil

1. Add salt to the beaten eggs and set aside for 10 minutes.
2. Heat your griddle to medium heat and add the bacon strips. Cook until most of the fat has rendered, but bacon is still flexible. Remove the bacon from the griddle and place on paper towels.
3. Once the bacon has drained, chop into small pieces.

4. Add the eggs to the griddle in two even pools. Cook until the bottom of the eggs starts to firm up. Add the gruyere to the eggs and cook until the cheese has started to melt and the eggs are just starting to brown.
5. Add the bacon pieces and use a spatula to turn one half of the omelet onto the other half. Remove from the griddle, season with pepper and chives and serve.

Potato Bacon Burrito with Avocado

Prep time: 5 minutes | Cook time: 20 minutes | Serves 2

4 eggs	½ yellow onion
4 strips bacon	1 ripe avocado, sliced
1 large russet potato, peeled and cut into small cubes	2 tablespoon hot sauce
1 red bell pepper	2 large flour tortillas
	Vegetable oil

1. Preheat the griddle to medium-high heat on one side and medium heat on the other side. Brush with vegetable oil and add the bacon to the medium heat side and peppers and onions to the medium-high side.
2. When the bacon finishes cooking, place on paper towels and chop into small pieces. Add the potatoes to the bacon fat on the griddle. Cook the potatoes until softened.
3. Add the eggs to the vegetable side and cook until firm. Place the ingredients onto the tortillas and top with slices of avocado and a tablespoon of hot sauce. Fold the tortillas and enjoy.

Turkey Cheese Panini with Pesto

Prep time: 5 minutes | Cook time: 6 minutes | Serves 2

1 tablespoon olive oil
4 slices French bread
½ cup pesto sauce
4 slices Mozzarella cheese

2 cups chopped leftover turkey
1 Roma tomato, thinly sliced
1 avocado, halved, seeded, peeled and sliced

1. Preheat griddle to medium-high heat.
2. Brush each slice of bread with olive oil on one side.
3. Place 2 slices olive oil side down on the griddle.
4. Spread 2 tablespoons pesto over 1 side of French bread.
5. Top with one slice Mozzarella, turkey, tomatoes, avocado, a second slice of Mozzarella, and top with second half of bread to make a sandwich; repeat with remaining slices of bread.
6. Cook until the bread is golden and the cheese is melted, about 2 to 3 minutes per side.
7. Serve warm with your favorite salad or soup.

Beef and Corn Burger

Prep time: 20 minutes | Cook time: 30 minutes | Serves 6

1 large egg, lightly beaten
1 cup whole kernel corn, cooked
½ cup bread crumbs
2 tablespoons shallots, minced
1 teaspoon Worcestershire sauce

2 pounds (907 g) ground beef
1 teaspoon salt
½ teaspoon pepper
½ teaspoon ground sage

1. Preheat griddle to medium heat.
2. Combine the egg, corn, bread crumbs, shallots, and Worcestershire sauce in a mixing bowl and set aside.
3. Combine ground beef and seasonings in a separate bowl.
4. Line a flat surface with waxed paper.
5. Roll beef mixture into 12 thin burger patties.
6. Spoon corn mixture into the center of 6 patties and spread evenly across within an inch of the edge.
7. Top each with a second circle of meat and press edges to seal corn mixture in the middle of each burger.
8. Cook for 12 to 15 minutes on each side or until thermometer reads 160ºF (71ºC) and juices run clear.

Tomato and Chicken Cheese Flatbreads

Prep time: 15 minutes | Cook time: 7 minutes | Serves 4

4 flat breads or thin pita bread
For the Topping:
1½ cups sliced grilled chicken, pre-cooked or leftovers
½ cup sun-dried tomatoes, coarsely chopped
6 leaves fresh basil, coarsely chopped
3 cups Mozzarella cheese, shredded

1 teaspoon salt
1 teaspoon ground black pepper
1 teaspoon red pepper flakes
Olive or chili oil, for serving

1. Preheat the griddle to low heat.
2. Mix all the topping ingredients together in a large mixing bowl with a rubber spatula.
3. Lay flatbreads on griddle, and top with an even amount of topping mixture; spreading to the edges of each.
4. Tent the flatbreads with foil for 5 minutes each, or until cheese is just melted.
5. Place flatbreads on a flat surface or cutting board, and cut each with a pizza cutter or kitchen scissors.
6. Drizzle with olive or chili oil to serve!

Golden Hash Brown

Prep time: 10 minutes | Cook time: 15 minutes | Serves 4

3 russet potatoes, peeled
1 tablespoon onion powder
1 tablespoon salt

1 teaspoon black pepper
Vegetable oil

1. Using the largest holes on a box grater, grate the potatoes and place in a large bowl. When all of the potatoes have been grated, rinse with water.
2. Squeeze as much water out of the potatoes as possible and return to the bowl.
3. Add the onion powder, salt, and pepper to the bowl and stir to combine.
4. Preheat your griddle to medium heat and add a think layer of oil. Spread the potato mixture onto the grill creating a layer about ½ inch thick. Cook for approximately 8 minutes.
5. Working in sections using a large spatula, turn the potatoes and cook an additional 5 to 8 minutes or until both sides are golden brown.
6. Remove the potatoes from the griddle in sections and add to plates. Sprinkle with a pinch of salt and serve immediately.

Potato Pancakes

Prep time: 5 minutes | Cook time: 8 minutes | Serves 2 to 4

2 eggs
¼ cup milk
1½ cups russet potato, peeled and shredded
¼ cup all-purpose flour
¼ cup finely diced onion

¼ cup finely chopped green onion
1 teaspoon baking powder
1 teaspoon salt
1 teaspoon pepper
Cooking oil, as needed

1. In a large bowl, beat the eggs and milk until frothy. Add the remaining ingredients and stir to combine. The batter should be moist throughout but not pooling with liquid. Allow to rest for 20 minutes while the grill heats up.
2. Bring the griddle grill to medium-high heat.
3. Add a thin coat of oil to the cooking surface, and when it begins to shimmer, add about ¼ cup of potato pancake batter to the griddle for each pancake. Press the batter to flatten and cook each side for 3 to 4 minutes until golden brown.

Chapter 2 Vegetables, Tofu and Fruit

Asparagus Spears with Butter

Prep time: 15 minutes | Cook time: 25 minutes | Serves 4 to 6

1½ pounds (680 g) thick asparagus spears, trimmed
3 tablespoons unsalt-
ed butter, melted
Salt and pepper, to taste

1. Preheat griddle to medium-high heat.
2. Brush asparagus with melted butter and season with salt and pepper.
3. Place asparagus in even layer on griddle and cook until just tender and browned, 4 to 10 minutes, turning halfway through cooking. Transfer asparagus to platter and serve.

Butternut Squash

Prep time: 6 minutes | Cook time: 10 minutes | Serves 4 to 6

1 small butternut squash (about 2 pounds / 907 g), peeled, seeded, and cut into ½-inch-thick
slices
Salt and pepper, to taste
3 tablespoons extra-virgin olive oil

1. Place squash slices in large pot. Cover with 2 quarts cold water. Add 1 teaspoon salt and bring to boil over high heat. Reduce heat to medium and simmer until squash is barely tender, about 3 minutes. Drain squash in colander, being careful not to break up squash slices. Transfer squash to large bowl; drizzle oil over top. Season with salt and pepper to taste, and gently turn squash to coat both sides of each slice with oil.
2. Preheat griddle to medium-high heat and brush with oil.
3. Place squash slices on griddle and cook, turning once, until dark brown caramelization occurs and flesh becomes very tender, 8 to 10 minutes. Serve hot, warm, or at room temperature.

Coleslaw with Carrot

Prep time: 9 minutes | Cook time: 15 minutes | Serves 4

½ (1-pound / 454-g) head green cabbage, cut into 2 wedges
2 tablespoons olive oil
Salt and pepper, to taste
¼ cup mayonnaise
1 shallot, minced
4 teaspoons cider vinegar
1 carrot, peeled and shredded
2 tablespoons minced fresh cilantro

1. Preheat griddle to medium-high heat. Brush cabbage wedges with oil and season with salt and pepper.
2. Place cabbage on griddle. Cook, turning as needed, until cabbage is lightly charred on all sides, 8 to 12 minutes. Transfer cabbage to platter; tent with aluminum foil and let rest.
3. Whisk mayonnaise, shallot, and vinegar together in large bowl. Slice cabbage into thin strips, discarding core. Stir cabbage, carrot, and cilantro into mayonnaise mixture. Season with salt and pepper to taste. Serve.

Grilled Corn

Prep time: 6 minutes | Cook time: 13 minutes | Serves 4 to 6

8 ears corn, husks and silk removed
2 tablespoons vege-
table oil
Salt and pepper, to taste

1. Place flavored butter in disposable pan. Brush corn evenly with oil and season with salt and pepper.
2. Preheat griddle to medium-high heat and brush with oil.
3. Place corn on griddle and cook, turning occasionally, until lightly charred on all sides, 5 to 9 minutes. Cover and cook until butter is sizzling, about 3 minutes. Remove pan from griddle and carefully remove foil, allowing steam to escape away from you. Serve corn, spooning any butter in pan over individual ears.

Bell Peppers with Garlic

Prep time: 20 minutes | Cook time: 50 minutes | Serves 4

¼ cup extra-virgin olive oil
3 garlic cloves, peeled and smashed
Salt and pepper, to taste
6 red bell peppers
1 tablespoon sherry vinegar

1. Combine oil, garlic, ½ teaspoon salt, and ¼ teaspoon pepper in bowl. Using paring knife, cut around stems of peppers and remove cores and seeds. Place peppers in bowl and turn to coat with oil. Cover bowl tightly with aluminum foil.
2. Preheat griddle to medium-high heat and brush with oil.
3. Place the peppers on griddle and cook, covered, until peppers are just tender and skins begin to blister, 10 to 15 minutes, rotating and shaking halfway through cooking.
4. Using tongs, remove peppers from griddle, allowing juices to drip back into bowl, and place on griddle. Cook peppers, covered, turning every few minutes until skins are blackened, 10 to 15 minutes.
5. Whisk juices and garlic in bowl with vinegar. Remove peppers from griddle, return to another bowl, and cover tightly with foil. Let peppers steam for 5 minutes. Using spoon, scrape blackened skin off each pepper. Quarter peppers lengthwise, add to vinaigrette in bowl, and toss to combine. Season with salt and pepper to taste, and serve.

Eggplant with Yogurt

Prep time: 13 minutes | Cook time: 30 minutes | Serves 6 to 8

6 tablespoons extra-virgin olive oil
5 garlic cloves, minced
⅛ teaspoon red pepper flakes
½ cup plain whole-milk yogurt
3 tablespoons minced fresh mint
1 teaspoon grated lemon zest plus 2 teaspoons juice
1 teaspoon ground cumin
Salt and pepper, to taste
2 pounds (907 g) eggplant, sliced into ¼-inch-thick rounds

1. Microwave oil, garlic, and pepper flakes in bowl until garlic is golden and crisp, about 2 minutes. Strain oil through fine-mesh strainer into clean bowl; reserve oil and crispy garlic mixture separately.
2. Combine 1 tablespoon strained garlic oil, yogurt, mint, lemon zest and juice, cumin, and ¼ teaspoon salt in bowl; set aside. Brush eggplant thoroughly with remaining garlic oil and season with salt and pepper.
3. Preheat griddle to medium-high heat.
4. Clean and oil your griddle. Place half of eggplant on griddle. Cook, turning as needed, until browned and tender, 8 to 10 minutes. Transfer to platter and repeat with remaining eggplant. Before serving, drizzle with yogurt sauce and sprinkle with crispy garlic mixture.

Garlicky Mushrooms

Prep time: 8 minutes | Cook time: 13 minutes | Serves 4 to 6

½ cup olive oil
3 tablespoons lemon juice
6 garlic cloves, minced
¼ teaspoon salt
4 portobello mushrooms (5 to 6 inches in diameter), stemmed

1. Combine oil, lemon juice, garlic, and salt in 1-gallon zipper-lock bag. Add mushrooms and toss to coat; press out as much air as possible and seal bag. Let sit at room temperature for 1 hour.
2. Meanwhile, cut four 12-inch square pieces of aluminum foil (or six 9-inch square pieces if using smaller mushrooms).
3. Preheat griddle to medium-high heat and brush with oil.
4. Remove mushrooms from marinade and place each on foil square, cook side up. Fold foil around each mushroom and seal edges. Place foil packets on griddle, sealed side up, and cook until juicy and tender, 9 to 12 minutes.
5. Using tongs, unwrap mushrooms, place gill side up on griddle, and cook for 30 to 60 seconds. Transfer to platter and serve.

Tomato and Zucchini Ratatouille

Prep time: 16 minutes | Cook time: 26 minutes | Serves 6 to 8

1 red onion, cut into ½-inch-thick slices and skewered
2 pounds (907 g) eggplant, sliced into ¾-inch-thick rounds
1½ pounds (680 g) zucchini or summer squash, sliced lengthwise into ½-inch-thick planks
2 bell peppers, stemmed, seeded, and halved, each half cut into thirds
1 pound (454 g) tomatoes, cored and halved
¼ cup extra-virgin olive oil, plus extra for brushing
Salt and pepper, to taste
3 tablespoons sherry vinegar
¼ cup chopped fresh basil
1 tablespoon minced fresh thyme
1 garlic clove, minced to paste

1. Place onion, eggplant, zucchini, bell peppers and tomatoes on baking sheet, brush with oil, and season with salt and pepper. Whisk ¼ cup oil, vinegar, basil, thyme, and garlic together in large bowl.
2. Preheat griddle to medium-high heat and brush with oil.
3. Place vegetables on griddle and cook, turning once, until tender, 10 to 12 minutes for onion, 8 to 10 minutes for eggplant and squash, 7 to 9 minutes for peppers, and 4 to 5 minutes for tomatoes. Remove vegetables from griddle as they are done and let cool slightly.
4. When cool enough to handle, chop vegetables into ½-inch pieces and add to oil mixture; toss to coat. Season with salt and pepper to taste, and serve warm or at room temperature.

Grilled Plantains

Prep time: 14 minutes | Cook time: 20 minutes | Serves 4

2 large ripe plantains
2 tablespoons vegetable oil
table oil
Salt, to taste

1. Trim ends from plantains, then cut crosswise into 4 pieces. With paring knife, make slit in peel of each piece, from 1 end to other end, and then peel away skin with your fingers. Cut each piece of plantain in half lengthwise. Place plantains in large bowl, add oil, season with salt, and gently toss to coat.
2. Preheat griddle to medium-high heat and brush with oil.
3. Place plantains on griddle and cook, turning once, until grill marks appear, 7 to 8 minutes.

Tofu with Cilantro

Prep time: 13 minutes | Cook time: 25 minutes | Serves 4 to 6

For the Glaze:
1/3 cup soy sauce
1/3 cup water
1/3 cup sugar
¼ cup mirin
1 tablespoon grated fresh ginger
2 garlic cloves, minced
2 teaspoons cornstarch
1 teaspoon Asian chili-garlic sauce

For the Tofu:
28 ounces (794 g) firm tofu, sliced lengthwise into 1-inch-thick planks
2 tablespoons vegetable oil
Salt and pepper, to taste
¼ cup minced fresh cilantro

1. Simmer soy sauce, water, sugar, mirin, ginger, garlic, cornstarch, and chili-garlic sauce on griddle over medium-high heat until thickened and reduced to ¾ cup, 5 to 7 minutes; transfer to bowl.
2. Spread tofu over paper towel, let drain for 20 minutes, then gently press dry with paper towels. Brush tofu with oil and season with salt and pepper.
3. Preheat griddle to high heat and brush with oil.
4. Gently place tofu on griddle. Cook until lightly browned on both sides, 6 to 10 minutes, gently flipping tofu halfway through cooking using 2 spatulas.
5. Turn the griddle to medium. Brush tofu with ¼ cup glaze and cook until well browned, 1 to 2 minutes. Flip tofu, brush with ¼ cup glaze, and cook until well browned, 1 to 2 minutes. Transfer tofu to platter, brush with remaining ¼ cup glaze, and sprinkle with cilantro. Serve.

Eggplant with Mole

Prep time: 25 minutes | Cook time: 40 minutes | Serves 6

For the Mole:

¼ cup coriander seeds
4 cloves
1 cinnamon stick
1 cup unsalted peanuts
½ cup raw pumpkin seeds (pepitas)
½ cup raw sunflower seeds
5 chipotle chiles, stemmed and seeded
4 guajillo chiles, stemmed and seeded
3 pasilla chiles, stemmed and seeded
2 ancho chiles, stemmed and seeded
2 ounces (57 g) dark chocolate (80% cacao or higher)
1 teaspoon dried oregano
1 head roasted garlic , cloves removed
1 white or red onion, quartered
3 ripe plantains, unpeeled
½ ripe pineapple, cored
¾ cup apple juice
¼ cup apple cider vinegar
½ cup honey
Salt, for seasoning
3 large globe eggplants
Oil, for coating

1. Preheat griddle to medium-high heat and brush with oil.
2. To make the mole: Cook the following ingredients in separate batches until fragrant and starting to turn color: coriander, cloves, and cinnamon; peanuts; pumpkin seeds and sunflower seeds; all chiles. As each batch cooks, transfer to a large bowl. Add the chocolate, oregano, and garlic.
3. Coat the onion in oil and cook over high heat until charred on all sides and tender throughout, 5 to 10 minutes. Transfer to a small bowl and cover with plastic wrap so it steams in its own heat, then add to the large bowl.
4. Cook the plantains over high heat until blackened and soft, about 10 minutes. Peel and add to the same large bowl. Slice the pineapple, coat with oil, and cook over high heat until deeply caramelized and softened, about 5 minutes. Add to the same large bowl.
5. Working in batches, transfer the contents of the large bowl to a blender along with the apple juice, cider vinegar, and honey, and blend until very smooth, adding just enough water to keep the blades turning. Strain through a fine-mesh strainer, pushing the mixture through with a rubber spatula.
6. Transfer the mole to the griddle and cook over medium heat for 15 minutes, adding more water if necessary to keep it at a saucy consistency. Season with salt before serving.
7. Slice each eggplant lengthwise into 1-inch-thick slices. Brush with oil and cook over medium heat until deep-brown appear and the eggplant is tender, 3 to 5 minutes per side. Serve with the mole.

Cabbage with Thyme

Prep time: 7 minutes | Cook time: 10 minutes | Serves 4

Salt and pepper, to taste
1 (2-pound/ 907-g) head green cabbage, cut into 8 wedges through core
1 tablespoon minced fresh thyme
2 teaspoons minced
shallot
2 teaspoons honey
1 teaspoon Dijon mustard
½ teaspoon grated lemon zest plus 2 tablespoons juice
6 tablespoons extra-virgin olive oil

1. Sprinkle 1 teaspoon salt evenly over cabbage wedges and let sit for 45 minutes. Combine thyme, shallot, honey, mustard, lemon zest and juice, and ¼ teaspoon pepper in bowl. Slowly whisk in oil until incorporated. Measure out ¼ cup vinaigrette and set aside.
2. Preheat griddle to medium-high heat and brush with oil.
3. Brush 1 cut side of cabbage wedges with half of vinaigrette. Place cabbage on griddle, vinaigrette side down, and cook until well browned, 7 to 10 minutes. Brush tops of wedges with remaining vinaigrette; flip and cook until second side is well browned and fork-tender, 7 to 10 minutes. Transfer cabbage to platter and drizzle with reserved vinaigrette. Season with salt and pepper to taste. Serve.

Potato Hobo Packs

Prep time: 16 minutes | Cook time: 30 minutes | Serves 4

2 pounds (907 g) Yukon Gold potatoes, unpeeled
1 tablespoon olive oil
2 garlic cloves, peeled and chopped
1 teaspoon minced fresh thyme
1 teaspoon salt
½ teaspoon pepper

1. Cut each potato in half crosswise, then cut each half into 8 wedges. Place potatoes in large bowl, cover, and microwave until edges of potatoes are translucent, 4 to 7 minutes, shaking bowl to redistribute potatoes halfway through microwaving. Drain well. Gently toss potatoes with oil, garlic, thyme, salt, and pepper.
2. Cut four 14 by 10-inch sheets of heavy-duty aluminum foil. Working with one at a time, spread one-quarter of potato mixture over half of foil, fold foil over potatoes, and crimp edges tightly to seal.
3. Preheat griddle to medium-high heat and brush with oil.
4. Place hobo packs on griddle and cook, covered, until potatoes are completely tender, about 10 minutes, flipping packs halfway through cooking. Cut open foil and serve.

Zucchini and Eggplant Salad

Prep time: 14 minutes | Cook time: 30 minutes | Serves 4 to 6

3 tablespoons white wine vinegar
3 garlic cloves, minced
1½ teaspoons Dijon mustard
Salt and pepper, to taste
6 tablespoons olive oil
3 (8-ounce / 227-g) zucchini, halved lengthwise
1 red onion, sliced into ½-inch-thick rounds
1 red bell pepper, stemmed, seeded, and halved lengthwise
1 pound (454 g) eggplant, sliced into ½-inch-thick rounds
3 tablespoons chopped fresh basil
1 tablespoon minced fresh parsley

1. Whisk vinegar, garlic, mustard, ½ teaspoon salt, and ½ teaspoon pepper together in large bowl. Slowly whisk in oil until thoroughly incorporated. Measure out 2 tablespoons dressing and set aside. Add zucchini, onion, and bell pepper to remaining dressing and turn to coat. Marinate vegetables for 15 minutes, tossing occasionally.
2. Preheat griddle to medium-high heat and brush with oil.
3. Place eggplant and marinated vegetables on griddle, beginning with eggplant. Cook until charred and tender, 4 to 6 minutes per side, removing eggplant last. Chop vegetables into 1-inch pieces and toss with reserved dressing, basil, and parsley. Let cool for 10 minutes. Season with salt and pepper to taste. Serve.

Broccoli Rice with Cilantro

Prep time: 7 minutes | Cook time: 16 minutes | Serves 4 to 6

6 large tomatillos, peeled and rinsed
Oil, for coating
1 white onion, coarsely chopped
2 cups cilantro (leaves and stems)
1 tablespoon roasted garlic
2 teaspoons salt, plus more for seasoning
1½ cups water
2 cups white rice
1 bunch scallions, bases trimmed
1 head broccoli, cut in half
1 cup basil leaves, coarsely chopped
1 cup parsley leaves, coarsely chopped

1. Preheat griddle to high heat and brush with oil.
2. Toss the tomatillos in enough oil to coat and cook over high heat until charred, about 5 minutes, turning often to char evenly. Transfer to a blender with the onion, 1 cup of the cilantro, the garlic, salt, and water and puree until smooth. Set aside.
3. Add the rice and cook, stirring constantly, until toasted and slightly translucent, about 3 minutes. Pour in the tomatillo puree and stir to combine. Cook, stirring only if necessary to avoid burning, until most of the liquid has been absorbed, 10 to 12 minutes. Cover and cook for 5 more minutes. Keeping the lid on, remove from the griddle and let it sit and steam until ready to serve.
4. While the rice cooks, toss the scallions and broccoli in enough oil to coat and cook over medium heat until charred but not burned, about 1 minute for the scallions and 5 minutes for the broccoli (lay the scallions crosswise on the griddle). Remove from the griddle and place both in a bowl, tightly cover, and let steam for 5 to 10 minutes.
5. Coarsely chop the scallions, broccoli, and the remaining 1 cup cilantro. Add to the rice together with the basil and parsley. Fluff with a fork, season with salt, and serve immediately.

Celery Horseradish Slaw

Prep time: 20 minutes | Cook time: 30 minutes | Serves 4 to 6

For the Horseradish Mayonnaise:
1 cup mayonnaise
¼ cup Dijon mustard
¼ cup freshly grated horseradish (may substitute store-bought horseradish)
¼ teaspoon salt
¼ teaspoon chile powder (ground cayenne pepper or chile de árbol)

For the Horseradish Slaw:
1 white onion, sliced paper thin and separated into rings
1 cup vinegar
1 tablespoon sugar
½ tablespoon salt
1 large celery root, peeled and cut in half
1 green apple
2 watermelon radishes (about 3 inches in diameter), peeled
1 cup celery leaves (may substitute parsley or chervil leaves)
1 cup coarsely chopped mixed fresh herbs, such as basil, dill, chives, and cilantro
2 tablespoons Pickled Mustard Seeds

1. In a small bowl, whisk together the mayonnaise, mustard, horseradish, salt, and chile powder until smooth. Store, covered, in the refrigerator for up to 2 days.
2. Place the onion in a bowl with the vinegar, sugar, and salt. Stir to dissolve the sugar and set aside to pickle for at least 30 minutes.
3. Using a mandoline or very sharp knife, slice the celery root as thinly as possible. Stack the slices and cut again lengthwise into thin strips. Do the same with the apple and the watermelon radishes. Immediately toss the celery root and apple with a little of the horseradish mayo to coat, so the cut surfaces don't turn brown. Add the drained pickled onions, celery leaves, herbs, mustard seeds, and the remaining mayo and toss well. Refrigerate, covered, for at least 1 hour and up to 2 days.

Mushroom Arugula Cheese Burgers

Prep time: 15 minutes | Cook time: 30 minutes | Serves 4

4 (4- to 5-inch) portobello mushroom caps, stems and gills removed
1 large red onion, sliced into ½-inch-thick rounds (do not separate rings)
3 tablespoons plus 1 teaspoon olive oil
Salt and pepper, to taste
2 garlic cloves, minced
2 teaspoons minced fresh thyme
2 ounces (57 g) goat cheese, crumbled (½ cup)
4 hamburger buns
1 cup baby arugula
¼ teaspoon balsamic vinegar
1 tomato, cored and sliced thin

1. Using tip of sharp knife, lightly score top of each mushroom cap in crosshatch pattern. Brush onion rounds with 1 tablespoon oil and season with salt and pepper. Combine 2 tablespoons oil, garlic, thyme, ¼ teaspoon salt, and ¼ teaspoon pepper in bowl.
2. Preheat griddle to medium-high heat and brush with oil.
3. Place mushrooms, gill side down, and onion rounds on griddle. Cook mushrooms until lightly charred and beginning to soften on gill side, 4 to 6 minutes. Flip mushrooms, brush with garlic-oil mixture, and cook until tender and browned on second side, 4 to 6 minutes. Sprinkle with goat cheese and let melt, about 2 minutes.
4. Meanwhile, cook onions, turning as needed, until spottily charred on both sides, 8 to 12 minutes. As they finish cooking, transfer mushrooms and onions to platter and tent with aluminum foil. Split hamburger buns open and grill until warm and lightly charred, about 30 seconds. Transfer to platter.
5. Toss arugula with balsamic vinegar and remaining 1 teaspoon oil in bowl and season with salt and pepper to taste. Separate onion rings. Assemble mushroom caps, arugula, tomato, and onion on buns and serve.

Red Potatoes with Rosemary

Prep time: 18 minutes | Cook time: 40 minutes | Serves 4

¼ cup olive oil
9 garlic cloves, minced
1 teaspoon chopped fresh rosemary
Salt and pepper, to taste
2 pounds (907 g) small red potatoes, unpeeled, halved, and threaded onto wooden skewers
2 tablespoons chopped fresh chives

1. Heat oil, garlic, rosemary, and ½ teaspoon salt on griddle over medium heat until sizzling, about 3 minutes. Reduce heat to medium-low and continue to cook until garlic is light blond, about 3 minutes. Pour mixture through fine-mesh strainer into small bowl; press on solids. Measure 1 tablespoon solids and 1 tablespoon oil into large bowl and set aside. Discard remaining solids but reserve remaining oil.
2. Place skewered potatoes in single layer on large plate and poke each potato several times with skewer. Brush with 1 tablespoon strained oil and season with salt. Microwave until potatoes offer slight resistance when pierced with paring knife, about 8 minutes, turning halfway through microwaving. Transfer potatoes to griddle coated with 1 tablespoon strained oil. Brush with remaining 1 tablespoon strained oil and season with salt and pepper to taste.
3. Preheat griddle to medium-high heat and brush with oil.
4. Place potatoes on griddle and cook for 3 to 5 minutes, flipping halfway through cooking. Turn the griddle to medium-low. Cover and continue to cook until paring knife slips in and out of potatoes easily, 5 to 8 minutes longer.
5. Remove potatoes from skewers and transfer to bowl with reserved garlic-oil mixture. Add chives, season with salt and pepper to taste, and toss until thoroughly coated. Serve.

Chapter 3 Poultry

Classic BBQ Chicken

Prep time: 5 minutes | Cook time: 1 hour 45 minutes | Serves 4-6

4 pounds (1.8 kg) of your favorite chicken, including legs, thighs, wings, and breasts, skin-on

Salt, to taste
Olive oil
1 cup barbecue sauce, like Hickory Mesquite or homemade

1. Rub the chicken with olive oil and salt.
2. Preheat the griddle to high heat.
3. Sear chicken skin side down on the grill for 5 to 10 minutes.
4. Turn the griddle down to medium low heat, tent with foil and cook for 30 minutes.
5. Turn chicken and baste with barbecue sauce.
6. Cover the chicken again and allow to cook for another 20 minutes.
7. Baste, cover and cook again for 30 minutes; repeat basting and turning during this time
8. The chicken is done when the internal temperature of the chicken pieces are 165ºF (74ºC) and juices run clear.
9. Baste with more barbecue sauce to serve

California Seared Chicken

Prep time: 15 minutes | Cook time: 20 minutes | Serves 4

4 boneless, skinless chicken breasts
¾ cup balsamic vinegar
2 tablespoons extra virgin olive oil

1 tablespoon honey
1 teaspoon oregano
1 teaspoon basil
1 teaspoon garlic powder

For Garnish

Sea salt
Black pepper, fresh ground
4 slices fresh mozzarella cheese

4 slices avocado
4 slices beefsteak tomato
Balsamic glaze, for drizzling

1. Whisk together balsamic vinegar, honey, olive oil, oregano, basil and garlic powder in a large mixing bowl.
2. Add chicken to coat and marinate for 30 minutes in the refrigerator.
3. Preheat griddle to medium-high. Sear chicken for 7 minutes per side, or until a meat thermometer reaches 165ºF (74ºC).
4. Top each chicken breast with mozzarella, avocado, and tomato and tent with foil on the griddle to melt for 2 minutes.
5. Garnish with a drizzle of balsamic glaze, and a pinch of sea salt and black pepper.

Salsa Verde Marinated Chicken

Prep time: 25 minutes| Cook time: 14 minutes | 6 Serves

6 boneless, skinless chicken breasts
1 tablespoon olive oil
1 teaspoon sea salt
1 teaspoon chili powder
1 teaspoon ground cumin
1 teaspoon garlic powder

For the Salsa Verde Marinade:

3 teaspoons garlic, minced
1 small onion, chopped
6 tomatillos, husked, rinsed and chopped
1 medium jalapeño pepper, cut in half, seeded
¼ cup fresh cilantro, chopped
½ teaspoon sugar or sugar substitute

1. Add salsa verde marinade ingredients to a food processor and pulse until smooth.
2. Mix sea salt, chili powder, cumin, and garlic powder together in a small mixing bowl. Season chicken breasts with olive oil and seasoning mix, and lay in glass baking dish.
3. Spread a tablespoon of salsa verde marinade over each chicken breast to cover; reserve remaining salsa for serving.
4. Cover dish with plastic wrap and refrigerate for 4 hours.
5. Preheat griddle to medium-high and brush with olive oil.
6. Add chicken to griddle and cook 7 minutes per side or until juices run clear and a meat thermometer reads 165ºF (74ºC).
7. Serve each with additional salsa verde and enjoy!

Sweet Chili Lime Chicken

Prep time: 15 minutes | Cook time: 15 minutes | Serves 4

½ cup sweet chili sauce
¼ cup soy sauce
1 teaspoon mirin
1 teaspoon orange juice, fresh squeezed
1 teaspoon orange marmalade
2 tablespoons lime juice
1 tablespoon brown sugar
1 clove garlic, minced
4 boneless, skinless chicken breasts
Sesame seeds, for garnish

1. Whisk sweet chili sauce, soy sauce, mirin, orange marmalade, lime and orange juice, brown sugar, and minced garlic together in a small mixing bowl.
2. Set aside ¼ cup of the sauce.
3. Toss chicken in sauce to coat and marinate 30 minutes.
4. Preheat your griddle to medium heat.
5. Put the chicken on the griddle and cook each side for 7 minutes.
6. Baste the cooked chicken with remaining marinade and garnish with sesame seeds to serve with your favorite sides

Seared Spicy Citrus Chicken

Prep time: 15 minutes | Cook time: 20 minutes | Serves 4

2 pounds (907 g) boneless, skinless chicken thighs
For the Marinade:
¼ cup fresh lime juice
2 teaspoon lime zest
¼ cup honey
2 tablespoons olive oil
1 tablespoon balsamic vinegar
½ teaspoon sea salt
½ teaspoon black pepper
2 garlic cloves, minced
¼ teaspoon onion powder

1. Whisk together marinade ingredients in a large mixing bowl; reserve 2 tablespoons of the marinade for basting.
2. Add chicken and marinade to a sealable plastic bag and marinate 8 hours or overnight in the refrigerator.
3. Preheat griddle to medium high heat and brush lightly with olive oil.

4. Place chicken on griddle and cook 8 minutes per side.
5. Baste each side of chicken with reserved marinade during the last few minutes of cooking; chicken is done when the internal temperature reaches 165ºF (74ºC).
6. Plate chicken, tent with foil, and allow to rest for 5 minutes.
7. Serve and enjoy!

Honey Sriracha Grilled Chicken Thighs

Prep time: 15 minutes | Cook time: 35 minutes | Serves 6

2½ pounds (1.1 kg) boneless chicken thighs
3 tablespoons butter, unsalted
1 tablespoon fresh ginger, minced
2 garlic cloves, minced
¼ teaspoon smoked paprika
¼ teaspoon chili powder
4 tablespoons honey
3 tablespoons Sriracha
1 tablespoon lime juice

1. Preheat griddle to medium high.
2. Melt butter in a small saucepan on medium low heat; when melted add ginger and garlic. Stir until fragrant, about 2 minutes.
3. Fold in smoked paprika, ground cloves, honey, Sriracha and lime juice. Stir to combine, turn heat to medium and simmer for 5 minutes.
4. Rinse and pat chicken thighs dry.
5. Season with salt and pepper on both sides.
6. Spray griddle with non-stick cooking spray.
7. Place chicken thighs on griddle, skin side down first. Grill for 5 minutes. Flip the chicken over and grill on the other side for 5 minutes.
8. Continue to cook chicken, flipping every 3 minutes, so it doesn't burn, until the internal temperature reads 165ºF on a meat thermometer.
9. During the last 5 minutes of grilling brush the glaze on both sides of the chicken.
10. Remove from griddle and serve warm

Chipotle Adobe Chicken

Prep time: 15 minutes | Cook time: 20 minutes | Serves 4 to 6

2 pounds (907 g) chicken thighs or breasts (boneless, skinless)

For the Marinade:
¼ cup olive oil
2 chipotle peppers, in adobo sauce, plus 1 teaspoon adobo sauce from the can
1 tablespoon garlic, minced
1 shallot, finely chopped
1½ tablespoons cumin
1 tablespoon cilantro, super-finely chopped or dried
2 teaspoons chili powder
1 teaspoon dried oregano
½ teaspoon salt
Fresh limes, garnish
Cilantro, garnish

1. Preheat griddle to medium-high.
2. Add marinade ingredients to a food processor or blender and pulse into a paste.
3. Add the chicken and marinade to a sealable plastic bag and massage to coat well.
4. Place in the refrigerator for 1 hour to 24 hours before cooking.
5. Sear chicken for 7 minutes, turn and cook and additional 7 minutes.
6. Turn heat to low and continue to cook until chicken has reached an internal temperature of 165ºF (74ºC).
7. Remove chicken from griddle and allow to rest 5 to 10 minutes before serving.
8. Garnish with a squeeze of fresh lime and a sprinkle of cilantro to serve.

Honey Balsamic Marinated Chicken

Prep time: 15 minutes | Cook time: 20 minutes | Serves 4

2 pounds (907 g) boneless, skinless chicken thighs
1 teaspoon olive oil
½ teaspoon sea salt
For the Marinade:
2 tablespoons honey
2 tablespoons balsamic vinegar
2 tablespoons tomato
¼ teaspoon black pepper
½ teaspoon paprika
¾ teaspoon onion powder

paste
1 teaspoon garlic, minced

1. Add chicken, olive oil, salt, black pepper, paprika, and onion powder to a sealable plastic bag. Seal and toss to coat, covering chicken with spices and oil; set aside.
2. Whisk together balsamic vinegar, tomato paste, garlic, and honey.
3. Divide the marinade in half. Add one half to the bag of chicken and store the other half in a sealed container in the refrigerator.
4. Seal the bag and toss chicken to coat. Refrigerate for 30 minutes to 4 hours.
5. Preheat a griddle to medium-high.
6. Discard bag and marinade. Add chicken to the griddle and cook 7 minutes per side or until juices run clear and a meat thermometer reads 165ºF (74ºC).
7. During last minute of cooking, brush remaining marinade on top of the chicken thighs & Serve immediately.

Hasselback Stuffed Chicken

Prep time: 15 minutes | Cook time: 30 minutes | Serves 4

4 boneless, skinless chicken breasts
2 tablespoons olive oil
2 tablespoons taco seasoning
½ red, yellow and green pepper, very thinly sliced
1 small red onion,
very thinly sliced
½ cup Mexican shredded cheese
Guacamole, for serving
Sour cream, for serving
Salsa, for serving

1. Preheat griddle to med-high.
2. Cut thin horizontal cuts across each chicken breast; like you would hasselback potatoes.
3. Rub chicken evenly with olive oil and taco seasoning.
4. Add a mixture of bell peppers and red onions to each cut, and place the breasts on the griddle.
5. Cook chicken for 15 minutes.
6. Remove and top with cheese.
7. Tent loosely with foil and cook another 5 minutes, until cheese is melted.
8. Remove from griddle and top with guacamole, sour cream and salsa. Serve alongside your favorite side dishes

Chicken Fried Rice

Prep time: 10 minutes| Cook time: 20 minutes | Serves 4

2 boneless, skinless chicken breasts, cut into small pieces
4 cups long grain rice, cooked and allowed to air dry
1/3 cup soy sauce
1 yellow onion, finely chopped
4 cloves garlic, finely chopped
1 cups petite peas
2 carrots sliced into thin rounds
½ cup corn kernels
¼ cup vegetable oil
2 tablespoons butter

1. Preheat griddle to medium-high.
2. Add the vegetable oil to the griddle.
3. When the oil is shimmering, add the onion, carrot, peas, and corn.
4. Cook for several minutes, until lightly charred.
5. Add the chicken and cook until just browned.
6. Add the rice, soy sauce, garlic, and butter.
7. Toss until the rice is tender and the vegetables are just softened.
8. Serve immediately.

Yellow Curry Chicken Wings

Prep time: 10 minutes | Cook time: 1 hour 30 minutes | Serves 6

2 pounds (907 g)   chicken wings
For the marinade:
½ cup Greek yogurt, plain
1 tablespoon mild yellow curry powder
1 tablespoon olive oil
½ teaspoon sea salt
½ teaspoon black pepper
1 teaspoon red chili flakes

1. Rinse and pat wings dry with paper towels.
2. Whisk marinade ingredients together in a large mixing bowl until well-combined.
3. Add wings to bowl and toss to coat.
4. Cover bowl with plastic wrap and chill in the refrigerator for 30 minutes.
5. Prepare one side of the griddle for medium heat and the other side on medium-high.
6. Working in batches, grill wings over medium heat, turning occasionally, until skin starts to brown; about 12 minutes.

7. Move wings to medium-high area of griddle for 5 minutes on each side to char until cooked through; meat thermometer should register 165ºF (74ºC) when touching the bone.
8. Transfer wings to a platter and serve warm.

Chicken Legs with Dates

Prep time: 15 minutes | Cook time: 40 minutes | Serves 4

4 skin-on chicken legs, including thighs
Salt, for coating
Onion and Smoked Date Jam
2 unpeeled red onions, halved
Oil, honey, and salt, for coating
6 pitted dates, smoked
½ cup sugar
1 cup vinegar
1 cup water

1. Preheat griddle to medium-high heat.
2. Rub the chicken legs with a light coating of salt and let them sit at room temperature for 30 minutes. (You can also refrigerate the chicken legs for up to 24 hours, but bring them to room temperature and wipe off the salt before grilling.)
3. To make the jam: Toss the onions in oil, honey, and salt to coat. Cook, cut side down, over medium heat until well charred, about 5 minutes. Transfer to a plate, set aside until cool enough to handle, then peel and thinly slice and add to a saucepan. Coarsely chop the dates and add to the saucepan along with the sugar, vinegar, and water. Place over medium heat and simmer until reduced and deeply caramelized, about 45 minutes.
4. While the jam reduces, grill the chicken legs over medium heat, turning every 5 minutes or so, until the skin is dark brown or until an instant-read meat thermometer placed in the thickest part of the thigh reads 180ºF (82ºC) (chicken legs and thighs are more tender when cooked to a higher temperature than chicken breasts). This should take 30 to 40 minutes total. Transfer to a cutting board and let rest for 10 minutes before cutting the thighs from the drumsticks. Serve immediately with the jam.

Korean Grilled Chicken Wings With Scallion

Prep time: 30 minutes | Cook time: 1 hour 30 minutes | Serves 6

2 pounds (907 g) chicken wings (flats and drumettes attached or separated)

For the Marinade:
1 tablespoon olive oil
1 teaspoon sea salt, plus more
½ teaspoon black pepper
½ cup gochujang, Korean hot pepper paste
1 scallion, thinly sliced, for garnish

1. Rinse and pat wings dry with paper towels.
2. Whisk marinade ingredients together in a large mixing bowl until well-combined.
3. Add wings to bowl and toss to coat.
4. Cover bowl with plastic wrap and chill in the refrigerator for 30 minutes.
5. Prepare one side of the griddle for medium heat and the other side on medium-high.
6. Working in batches, cook wings over medium heat, turning occasionally, until skin starts to brown; about 12 minutes.
7. Move wings to medium-high area of griddle for 5 minutes on each side to sear until cooked through; meat thermometer should register 165ºF (74ºC) when touching the bone.
8. Transfer wings to a platter, garnish with scallions, and serve warm with your favorite dipping sauces.

Creole Chicken Stuffed with Cheese and Peppers

Prep time: 10 minutes | Cook time: 20 minutes | Serves 4

4 boneless, skinless chicken breasts
8 mini sweet peppers, sliced thin and seeded
2 slices pepper jack cheese, cut in half
2 slices colby jack cheese, cut in half
1 tablespoon creole seasoning, like Emeril's
1 teaspoon black pepper
1 teaspoon garlic powder
1 teaspoon onion powder
4 teaspoons olive oil, separated
Toothpicks

1. Rinse chicken and pat dry.
2. Mix creole seasoning, pepper, garlic powder, and onion powder together in a small mixing bowl and set aside.
3. Cut a slit on the side of each chicken breast; be careful not to cut all the way through the chicken.
4. Rub each breast with 1 teaspoon each of olive oil.
5. Rub each chicken breast with seasoning mix and coat evenly.
6. Stuff each breast of chicken with 1 half pepper jack cheese slice, 1 half colby cheese slice, and a handful of pepper slices.
7. Secure chicken shut with 4 or 5 toothpicks.
8. Preheat the griddle to medium-high and cook chicken for 8 minutes per side; or until chicken reaches an internal temperature of 165ºF (74ºC).
9. Allow chicken to rest for 5 minutes, remove toothpicks, and serve.

Sweet Red Chili And Peach Glaze Wings

Prep time: 15 minutes | Cook time: 30 minutes | Serves 4

1 (12-ounce / 340-g) jar peach preserves
1 cup sweet red chili sauce
1 teaspoon lime juice
1 tablespoon fresh
cilantro, minced
1 (2½-pound / 1.1-kg) bag chicken wing sections
Non-stick cooking spray

1. Mix preserves, red chili sauce, lime juice and cilantro in mixing bowl. Divide in half, and place one half aside for serving.
2. Preheat griddle to medium heat and spray with non-stick cooking spray.
3. Cook wings for 25 minutes turning several times until juices run clear.
4. Remove wings from griddle, toss in a bowl to coat wings with remaining glaze.
5. Return wings to griddle and cook for an additional 3 to 5 minutes turning once.
6. Serve warm with your favorite dips and side dishes!

Root Beer Can Chicken

Prep time: 10 minutes | Cook time: 20 minutes | Serves 2 to 4

1 pounds (454 g) boneless chicken thighs	g) cans root beer, like A&W
3 (12-ounce / 340-	Olive oil

For the Rub:

1 tablespoon garlic powder	2 teaspoons garlic powder
¾ tablespoon sea salt	1 teaspoon dried thyme
½ tablespoon white pepper	⅛ teaspoon cayenne pepper
2 teaspoons smoked paprika	

1. Combine rub ingredients in a bowl; reserve half in a separate air tight container until ready to cook.
2. Rub chicken thighs evenly with olive oil and coat each with some rub.
3. Lay chicken in a 13 by 9 inch baking dish. Cover with 2 cans of root beer.
4. Preheat grill to medium-high heat.
5. Discard marinade and brush grill with olive oil.
6. Gently fold remaining rub and a half of the third can of root beer in a small bowl.
7. Sear chicken for 7 minutes on each side, basting often with root beer rub mix.
8. Serve when cooked through or chicken reaches 165ºF (74ºC).

Sizzling Chicken Fajitas

Prep time: 15 minutes | Cook time: 25 minutes | Serves 4

4 boneless chicken breast halves, thinly sliced	1 teaspoon onion powder
1 yellow onion, sliced	2 tablespoons lime juice
1 large green bell pepper, sliced	1 tablespoon olive oil
1 large red bell pepper, sliced	½ teaspoon black pepper
1 teaspoon ground cumin	1 teaspoon salt
1 teaspoon garlic powder	3 tablespoons vegetable oil
	10 flour tortillas

1. In a zipperlock bag, combine the chicken, cumin, garlic, onion, lime juice, salt, pepper, and olive oil. Allow to marinate for 30 minutes.
2. Preheat griddle to medium heat.
3. On one side of the griddle add the olive oil and heat until shimmering. Add the onion and pepper and cook until slightly softened.
4. On the other side of the griddle add the marinated chicken and cook until lightly browned.
5. Once chicken is lightly browned, toss together with the onion and pepper and cook until chicken registers 165ºF (74ºC).
6. Remove chicken and vegetables from the griddle and serve with warm tortillas.

Teriyaki Chicken and Veggie Rice Bowls

Prep time: 10 minutes| Cook time: 20 minutes | Serves 4

1 bag brown rice

For the Skewers:

2 boneless skinless chicken breasts, cubed	cube slices
	1 green pepper, cut into cube slices
1 red onion, quartered	½ pineapple, cut into cubes
1 red pepper, cut into	

For the Marinade:

¼ cup light soy sauce	fresh grated
¼ cup sesame oil	1 garlic clove, crushed
1 tablespoon ginger,	½ lime, juiced

1. Whisk the marinade ingredients together in a small mixing bowl.
2. Add chicken and marinade to a resealable plastic bag, seal and toss well to coat.
3. Refrigerate for one hour or overnight.
4. Prepare rice as instructed on the bag.
5. Preheat the griddle to medium-high heat.
6. Thread the chicken and the cubed veggies onto 8 metal skewers and cook for 8 minutes on each side until seared and cooked through.
7. Portion rice out into bowls and top with two skewers each, and enjoy!

Chicken Things with Ginger-Sesame Glaze

Prep time: 10 minutes | Cook time: 20 minutes | Serves 4-8

8 boneless, skinless chicken thighs
For the Glaze:

3 tablespoons dark brown sugar	1 teaspoon fresh ginger, minced
2½ tablespoons soy sauce	1 teaspoon sambal oelek
1 tablespoon fresh garlic, minced	⅓ cup scallions, thinly sliced
2 teaspoons sesame seeds	Non-stick cooking spray

1. Combine glaze ingredients in a large mixing bowl; separate and reserve half for serving.
2. Add chicken to bowl and toss to coat well.
3. Preheat the griddle to medium-high heat.
4. Coat with cooking spray.
5. Cook chicken for 6 minutes on each side or until done.
6. Transfer chicken to plates and drizzle with remaining glaze

Chicken with Mustard

Prep time: 15 minutes | Cook time: 40 minutes | Serves 4 to 6

2 (3- to 4-pound / 1.4- to 1.8-kg) whole chickens
For the Brine:

½ cup salt	Oil, for coating
½ cup sugar	Salt and pepper, for coating
8 cups water	
Toasted Mustard Seed	

1. Preheat griddle to medium-high heat.
2. To prepare each chicken, using kitchen shears, cut along both sides of the back bone and remove (your butcher can also do this for you). Place the chicken skin side up on the cutting board and apply firm pressure to the breastbone to flatten.
3. To make the brine: Combine the salt, sugar, and water and stir until dissolved. In a large bowl or stockpot, submerge the chickens in the liquid and refrigerate, covered, for at least 4 hours or up to overnight. Remove and pat dry.
4. Coat the chickens with the mustard seed oil, salt, and pepper and cook, bone side down, over high heat for about 10 minutes. Flip the chickens, move to medium heat, and cook for another 30 minutes, or until an instant-read meat thermometer placed in the thickest part of the thigh reads 165ºF (74ºC). Flip the chickens occasionally and baste with more mustard seed oil, if needed. Transfer to a cutting board and let the chickens rest for 10 minutes before carving into serving pieces.

Chicken with Salsa

Prep time: 25 minutes | Cook time: 5 hours | Serves 6

6 boneless, skinless chicken breasts	der
1 tablespoon olive oil	1 teaspoon ground cumin
1 teaspoon sea salt	1 teaspoon garlic powder
1 teaspoon chili pow-	

For the Salsa Verde Marinade:

3 teaspoons garlic, minced	pepper, cut in half, seeded
1 small onion, chopped	¼ cup fresh cilantro, chopped
6 tomatillos, husked, rinsed and chopped	½ teaspoon sugar or sugar substitute
1 medium jalapeño	

1. Add salsa verde marinade ingredients to a food processor and pulse until smooth.
2. Mix sea salt, chili powder, cumin, and garlic powder together in a small mixing bowl. Season chicken breasts with olive oil and seasoning mix, and lay in glass baking dish.
3. Spread a tablespoon of salsa verde marinade over each chicken breast to cover; reserve remaining salsa for serving.
4. Cover dish with plastic wrap and refrigerate for 4 hours.
5. Preheat griddle to medium-high and brush with olive oil.
6. Add chicken to griddle and cook 7 minutes per side or until juices run clear and a meat thermometer reads 165ºF (74ºC).
7. Serve each with additional salsa verde and enjoy!

Chicken with Cheese

Prep time: 35 minutes | Cook time: 20 minutes | Serves 4

4 boneless, skinless chicken breasts
¾ cup balsamic vinegar
2 tablespoons extra virgin olive oil
For Garnish:
Sea salt, to taste
Black pepper, fresh ground
4 slices fresh Mozzarella cheese

1 tablespoon honey
1 teaspoon oregano
1 teaspoon basil
1 teaspoon garlic powder

4 slices avocado
4 slices beefsteak tomato
Balsamic glaze, for drizzling

1. Whisk together balsamic vinegar, honey, olive oil, oregano, basil and garlic powder in a large mixing bowl.
2. Add chicken to coat and marinate for 30 minutes in the refrigerator.
3. Preheat griddle to medium-high. Sear chicken for 7 minutes per side, or until a meat thermometer reaches 165ºF (74ºC).
4. Top each chicken breast with Mozzarella, avocado, and tomato and tent with foil on the griddle to melt for 2 minutes.
5. Garnish with a drizzle of balsamic glaze, and a pinch of sea salt and black pepper.

Chicken Breasts with Chili Sauce

Prep time: 15 minutes | Cook time: 15 minutes | Serves 4

½ cup sweet chili sauce
¼ cup soy sauce
1 teaspoon mirin
1 teaspoon orange juice, fresh squeezed
1 teaspoon orange marmalade
2 tablespoons lime

juice
1 tablespoon brown sugar
1 clove garlic, minced
4 boneless, skinless chicken breasts
Sesame seeds, for garnish

1. Whisk sweet chili sauce, soy sauce, mirin, orange marmalade, lime and orange juice, brown sugar, and minced garlic together in a small mixing bowl.
2. Set aside ¼ cup of the sauce.

3. Toss chicken in sauce to coat and marinate 30 minutes.
4. Preheat your griddle to medium heat.
5. Put the chicken on the griddle and cook each side for 7 minutes.
6. Baste the cooked chicken with remaining marinade and garnish with sesame seeds to serve with your favorite sides.

Pepper and Cheese Stuffed Chicken

Prep time: 10 minutes | Cook time: 20 minutes | Serves 4

4 boneless, skinless chicken breasts
8 mini sweet peppers, sliced thin and seeded
2 slices Pepper Jack cheese, cut in half
2 slices colby jack cheese, cut in half
1 tablespoon creole

seasoning, like Emeril's
1 teaspoon black pepper
1 teaspoon garlic powder
1 teaspoon onion powder
4 teaspoons olive oil, separated

1. Rinse chicken and pat dry.
2. Mix creole seasoning, pepper, garlic powder, and onion powder together in a small mixing bowl and set aside.
3. Cut a slit on the side of each chicken breast; be careful not to cut all the way through the chicken.
4. Rub each breast with 1 teaspoon each of olive oil.
5. Rub each chicken breast with seasoning mix and coat evenly.
6. Stuff each breast of chicken with 1 half Pepper Jack cheese slice, 1 half colby cheese slice, and a handful of pepper slices.
7. Secure chicken shut with 4 or 5 toothpicks.
8. Preheat the griddle to medium-high and cook chicken for 8 minutes per side; or until chicken reaches an internal temperature of 165ºF (74ºC).
9. Allow chicken to rest for 5 minutes, remove toothpicks, and serve.

Buffalo Chicken Wings

Prep time: 10 minutes | Cook time: 20 minutes | Serves 6-8

1 tablespoon sea salt
1 teaspoon ground black pepper
1 teaspoon garlic powder
3 pounds (1.4 kg) chicken wings

6 tablespoons unsalted butter
1/3 cup buffalo sauce, like Moore's
1 tablespoon apple cider vinegar
1 tablespoon honey

1. Combine salt, pepper and garlic powder in a large mixing bowl.
2. Toss the wings with the seasoning mixture to coat.
3. Preheat griddle to medium heat.
4. Place the wings on the griddle; make sure they are touching so the meat stays moist on the bone while grilling.
5. Flip wings every 5 minutes, for a total of 20 minutes of cooking.
6. Heat the butter, buffalo sauce, vinegar and honey in a saucepan over low heat; whisk to combine well.
7. Add wings to a large mixing bowl, toss the wings with the sauce to coat.
8. Turn griddle up to medium high and place wings back on the griddle until the skins crisp; about 1 to 2 minutes per side.
9. Add wings back into the bowl with the sauce and toss to serve.

Kale Caesar Salad with Seared Chicken

Prep time: 10 minutes | Cook time: 8 minutes | Serves 1

1 chicken breast
1 teaspoon garlic powder
1/2 teaspoon black pepper

1/2 teaspoon sea salt
2 kale leaves, chopped
Shaved parmesan, for serving

For the Dressing:
1 tablespoon mayonnaise
1/2 tablespoon dijon mustard
1/2 teaspoon garlic powder
1/2 teaspoon worces-

tershire sauce
1/4 lemon, juice of (or 1/2 a small lime)
1/4 teaspoon anchovy paste
Pinch of sea salt
Pinch of black pepper

1. Mix garlic powder, black pepper, and sea salt in a small mixing bowl. Coat chicken with seasoning mix.
2. Preheat griddle to medium-high heat.
3. Sear chicken on each side for 7 minutes or until a meat thermometer reads 165ºF (74ºC) when inserted in the thickest part of the breast.
4. Whisk all of the dressing ingredients together.
5. Plate your kale and pour the dressing over, and toss to combine.
6. Cut the chicken on a diagonal and place on top of the salad. Garnish with shaved parmesan, and serve

Chicken Fajitas

Prep time: 5 minutes | Cook time: 25 minutes | Serves 4

4 boneless chicken breast halves, thinly sliced
1 yellow onion, sliced
1 large green bell pepper, sliced
1 large red bell pepper, sliced
1 teaspoon ground cumin
1 teaspoon garlic powder

1 teaspoon onion powder
2 tablespoons lime juice
1 tablespoon olive oil
1/2 teaspoon black pepper
1 teaspoon salt
3 tablespoons vegetable oil
10 flour tortillas

1. In a zipperlock bag, combine the chicken, cumin, garlic, onion, lime juice, salt, pepper, and olive oil. Allow to marinate for 30 minutes.
2. Preheat griddle to medium heat.
3. On one side of the griddle add the olive oil and heat until shimmering. Add the onion and pepper and cook until slightly softened.
4. On the other side of the griddle add the marinated chicken and cook until lightly browned.
5. Once chicken is lightly browned, toss together with the onion and pepper and cook until chicken registers 165ºF (74ºC).
6. Remove chicken and vegetables from the griddle and serve with warm tortillas.

Chicken Breasts with Cheese

Prep time: 15 minutes | Cook time: 30 minutes | Serves 4

4 boneless, skinless chicken breasts
2 tablespoons olive oil
2 tablespoons taco seasoning
½ red, yellow and green pepper, very thinly sliced
1 small red onion, very thinly sliced
½ cup Mexican shredded cheese
Guacamole, for serving
Sour cream, for serving
Salsa, for serving

1. Preheat griddle to med-high.
2. Cut thin horizontal cuts across each chicken breast; like you would hasselback potatoes.
3. Rub chicken evenly with olive oil and taco seasoning.
4. Add a mixture of bell peppers and red onions to each cut, and place the breasts on the griddle.
5. Cook chicken for 15 minutes.
6. Remove and top with cheese.
7. Tent loosely with foil and cook another 5 minutes, until cheese is melted.
8. Remove from griddle and top with guacamole, sour cream and salsa. Serve alongside your favorite side dishes!

Chicken Thighs with Scallions

Prep time: 10 minutes | Cook time: 20 minutes | Serves 4 to 8

8 boneless, skinless chicken thighs
For the glaze:
3 tablespoons dark brown sugar
2½ tablespoons soy sauce
1 tablespoon fresh garlic, minced
2 teaspoons sesame seeds
1 teaspoon fresh ginger, minced
1 teaspoon sambal oelek
⅓ cup scallions, thinly sliced
Non-stick cooking spray

1. Combine glaze ingredients in a large mixing bowl; separate and reserve half for serving.
2. Add chicken to bowl and toss to coat well.

3. Preheat the griddle to medium-high heat.
4. Coat with cooking spray.
5. Cook chicken for 6 minutes on each side or until done.
6. Transfer chicken to plates and drizzle with remaining glaze to serve.

Chicken Skewers with Cheese

Prep time: 20 minutes | Cook time: 20 minutes | Serves 2 to 4

10 boneless, skinless chicken thighs, cut into chunks
1 large red onion, cut into wedges
1 large red pepper, stemmed, seeded, and cut into chunks
For the Marinade:
⅓ cup toasted pine nuts
1½ cups sliced roasted red peppers
5 hot cherry peppers, stemmed and seeded, or to taste
1 cup packed fresh basil leaves, plus more to serve
4 cloves garlic, peeled
¼ cup grated Parmesan cheese
1 tablespoon paprika
Extra virgin olive oil, as needed

1. Combine the toasted pine nuts, roasted red peppers, hot cherry peppers, basil, garlic, Parmesan, and paprika in a food processor or blender and process until well-combined.
2. Add in olive oil until the pesto reaches a thin consistency in order to coat the chicken as a marinade.
3. Transfer half of the pesto to a large sealable plastic bag, and reserve the other half for serving.
4. Add the chicken thigh chunks to the bag of pesto, seal, and massage the bag to coat the chicken.
5. Refrigerate for 1 hour.
6. Preheat griddle to medium-high heat and brush with olive oil.
7. Thread the chicken cubes, red onion, and red pepper onto metal skewers.
8. Brush the chicken with the reserved pesto.
9. Cook until the chicken reaches an internal temperature of 165ºF (74ºC); about 5 minutes per side. Serve warm with your favorite salad or vegetables!

Chicken Wings Buffalo

Prep time: 10 minutes | Cook time: 20 minutes | Serves 6 to 8

1 tablespoon sea salt
1 teaspoon ground black pepper
1 teaspoon garlic powder
3 pounds (1.4 kg) chicken wings
6 tablespoons unsalted butter
1/3 cup buffalo sauce, like Moore's
1 tablespoon apple cider vinegar
1 tablespoon honey

1. Combine salt, pepper and garlic powder in a large mixing bowl.
2. Toss the wings with the seasoning mixture to coat.
3. Preheat griddle to medium heat.
4. Place the wings on the griddle; make sure they are touching so the meat stays moist on the bone while grilling.
5. Flip wings every 5 minutes, for a total of 20 minutes of cooking.
6. Heat the butter, buffalo sauce, vinegar and honey in a saucepan over low heat; whisk to combine well.
7. Add wings to a large mixing bowl, toss the wings with the sauce to coat.
8. Turn griddle up to medium high and place wings back on the griddle until the skins crisp; about 1 to 2 minutes per side.
9. Add wings back into the bowl with the sauce and toss to serve.

Chicken Wings with Yogurt

Prep time: 30 minutes | Cook time: 1/2 to 1 hour | Serves 6

2 pounds (907 g) chicken wings
For the Marinade:
1/2 cup Greek yogurt, plain
1 tablespoon mild yellow curry powder
1 tablespoon olive oil
1/2 teaspoon sea salt
1/2 teaspoon black pepper
1 teaspoon red chili flakes

1. Rinse and pat wings dry with paper towels.
2. Whisk marinade ingredients together in a large mixing bowl until well-combined.
3. Add wings to bowl and toss to coat.
4. Cover bowl with plastic wrap and chill in the refrigerator for 30 minutes.

5. Prepare one side of the griddle for medium heat and the other side on medium-high.
6. Working in batches, grill wings over medium heat, turning occasionally, until skin starts to brown; about 12 minutes.
7. Move wings to medium-high area of griddle for 5 minutes on each side to char until cooked through; meat thermometer should register 165ºF (74ºC) when touching the bone.
8. Transfer wings to a platter and serve warm.

Chicken Breasts

Prep time: 10 minutes | Cook time: 20 minutes | Serves 4

Salt and pepper, to taste
4 (10- to 12-ounce / 283- to 340-g)
bone-in split chicken breasts, trimmed
1 recipe glaze

1. Dissolve 1/2 cup salt in 2 quarts cold water in large container. Submerge chicken breasts in brine, cover, and refrigerate for 30 minutes to 1 hour. Remove chicken from brine and pat dry with paper towels. Season chicken with pepper.
2. Preheat griddle to medium-high heat and brush with oil.
3. Place chicken on griddle, skin side up, and cook until lightly browned on both sides, 6 to 8 minutes. Move chicken, skin side down, to cooler side of griddle, with thicker end of breasts facing hotter side. Cover loosely with aluminum foil. Cover and continue to cook until chicken registers 150ºF (66ºC), 15 to 20 minutes longer.
4. Brush bone side of chicken generously with half of glaze, and cook until browned, 5 to 10 minutes. Brush skin side of chicken with remaining glaze, flip chicken, and continue to cook until chicken registers 160ºF (71ºC), 2 to 3 minutes longer.
5. Transfer chicken to serving platter, tent with aluminum foil, and let rest for 5 to 10 minutes before serving, passing reserved glaze separately.

Chicken Wings with Pepper

Prep time: 15 minutes | Cook time: 40 minutes | Makes 2 dozen wings

½ cup salt
2 pounds (907 g) chicken wings, wingtips discarded, trimmed
1½ teaspoons cornstarch
1 teaspoon pepper

1. Dissolve salt in 2 quarts cold water in large container. Prick chicken wings all over with fork. Submerge chicken in brine, cover, and refrigerate for 30 minutes.
2. Combine cornstarch and pepper in bowl. Remove chicken from brine and pat dry with paper towels. Transfer wings to large bowl and sprinkle with cornstarch mixture, tossing until evenly coated.
3. Preheat griddle to medium-high heat and brush with oil.
4. Cook wings, thicker skin side up, until browned on bottom, 12 to 15 minutes. Flip chicken and grill until skin is crisp and lightly charred and meat registers 180ºF (82ºC), about 10 minutes. Transfer chicken to platter, tent with aluminum foil, and let rest for 5 to 10 minutes. Serve.

Seared Chicken With Fruit Salsa

Prep time: 25 minutes | Cook time: 20 minutes | Serves 4

4 boneless, skinless chicken breasts
For the Marinade:
½ cup fresh lemon juice
½ cup soy sauce
1 tablespoon fresh ginger, minced
1 tablespoon lemon pepper seasoning
2 garlic cloves, minced
For the Salsa:
1½ cups pineapple, chopped
¾ cup kiwi fruit, chopped
½ cup mango, chopped
½ cup red onion, finely chopped
2 tablespoons fresh cilantro, chopped
1 small jalapeño
pepper, seeded and chopped
1 ½ teaspoons ground cumin
¼ teaspoon sea salt
⅛ teaspoon black pepper
½ teaspoon olive oil, more for brushing griddle

1. Combine marinade ingredients in a large sealable plastic bag.
2. Add chicken to bag, seal, and toss to coat. Marinate in refrigerator for 1 hour.
3. Combine salsa ingredients in a mixing bowl and toss gently to combine. Set aside until ready to serve.
4. Preheat the griddle to medium heat.
5. Remove chicken from bag and discard marinade.
6. Brush griddle with olive oil and cook chicken for 7 minutes on each side or until chicken is cooked through.
7. Serve chicken topped with salsa alongside your favorite side dishes.

Spicy Chicken Wings

Prep time: 10 minutes | Cook time: ½ to 1 hour | Serves 6

2 pounds (907 g) chicken wings (flats and drumettes attached or separated)
For the Marinade:
1 tablespoon olive oil
1 teaspoon sea salt, plus more
½ teaspoon black pepper
½ cup gochujang, Korean hot pepper paste
1 scallion, thinly sliced, for garnish

1. Rinse and pat wings dry with paper towels.
2. Whisk marinade ingredients together in a large mixing bowl until well-combined.
3. Add wings to bowl and toss to coat.
4. Cover bowl with plastic wrap and chill in the refrigerator for 30 minutes.
5. Prepare one side of the griddle for medium heat and the other side on medium-high.
6. Working in batches, cook wings over medium heat, turning occasionally, until skin starts to brown; about 12 minutes.
7. Move wings to medium-high area of griddle for 5 minutes on each side to sear until cooked through; meat thermometer should register 165ºF (74ºC) when touching the bone.
8. Transfer wings to a platter, garnish with scallions, and serve warm with your favorite dipping sauces.

Chicken Satay with Almond Butter Sauce

Prep time: 30 minutes| Cook time: 8 minutes | Serves 4

1 pounds (454 g) boneless, skinless Olive oil, for brushing	chicken thighs, cut into thin strips

For the Marinade:

½ cup canned light coconut milk	flakes
½ lime, juiced	2 teaspoons ginger, grated
1 tablespoon honey	1 clove of garlic, grated
2 teaspoons soy sauce	½ teaspoon curry powder
1½ teaspoons fish sauce	¼ teaspoon ground coriander
½ teaspoon red chili	

For the Almond Butter Sauce:

¼ cup almond butter	1 teaspoon fish sauce
¼ cup water	1 teaspoon fresh grated ginger
2 tablespoons canned, light coconut milk	½ teaspoon low sodium soy sauce
1 tablespoon honey	½ teaspoon Sriracha
½ lime, juiced	

1. Whisk together all of the ingredients for the marinade in a medium mixing bowl.
2. Add chicken to mixing bowl and toss to coat.
3. Cover and refrigerate 2 hours or overnight.
4. Preheat griddle to medium high heat and brush with olive oil.
5. Thread the chicken strips onto metal skewers.
6. Place the chicken skewers on the prepared griddle and cook 3 minutes, rotate, and cook another 4 minutes or until the chicken is cooked through.
7. Whisk together all of the ingredients for the almond butter sauce in a small saucepan.
8. Bring the sauce to a boil on medium heat, then lower to medium low and simmer for 1 to 2 minutes or until the sauce thickens.
9. Serve chicken satay warm with the almond butter sauce and enjoy.

Vinegary Chicken with Mustard

Prep time: 15 minutes | Cook time: 40 minutes | Serves 4 to 6

2 (3- to 4-pound / 1.4- to 1.8-kg) whole chickens	3 tablespoons honey, plus more for basting and*to taste
2 cups pickled mustard seeds	2 teaspoons salt, plus more for seasoning
¼ cup vinegar	

1. Preheat griddle to medium-high heat.
2. To prepare each chicken, using kitchen shears, cut along both sides of the backbone and remove (your butcher can also do this for you). Place the chicken skin side up on the cutting board and apply firm pressure to the breastbone to flatten.
3. Add 1 cup of the mustard seeds to a blender together with the vinegar, 1 tablespoon of the honey, and the salt, and blend until smooth. Toss the chicken with the marinade and refrigerate, covered, for at least 2 hours or up to overnight. Remove the chicken from the marinade, wiping off any excess, and discard the marinade.
4. Cook the chickens, bone side down, over high heat for about 10 minutes. Flip the chickens, move to medium heat, and cook for another 30 minutes, or until an instant-read meat thermometer placed in the thickest part of the thigh reads 165ºF (74ºC). You can flip the chickens occasionally while cooking to give even color. During the last 5 minutes of cooking, brush them with honey. Transfer to a cutting board and let the chickens rest for 10 minutes before carving into serving pieces.
5. While the chickens are cooking, add the remaining 1 cup mustard seeds and the remaining 2 tablespoons honey to the blender and blend until smooth. Add additional honey and/or salt, if needed. To serve, smear the mustard seed puree on a large platter (or on 4 individual plates) and top with the chicken.

Chicken Tacos with Avocado Crema

Prep time: 25 minutes | Cook time: 10 minutes | Serves 4 to 5

1 (½-pound / 227-g) Boneless, skin- less chicken breasts, sliced thin

For the Chicken Marinade:

1 serrano pepper, minced

2 teaspoons garlic, minced

1 lime, juiced

1 teaspoon ground cumin

⅓ cup olive oil

Sea salt, to taste

Black pepper, to taste

For the Avocado Crema:

1 cup sour cream

2 teaspoons lime juice

1 teaspoon lime zest

1 serrano pepper, diced and seeded

1 clove garlic, minced

1 large hass avocado

The Garnish:

½ cup queso fresco, crumbled

2 teaspoons cilantro, chopped

1 lime sliced into wedges

10 corn tortillas

1. Mix chicken marinade together in a sealable plastic bag. Add chicken and toss to coat well.
2. Marinate for 1 hour in the refrigerator.
3. Combine avocado crema ingredients in a food processor or blender and pulse until smooth.
4. Cover and refrigerate until you are ready to assemble tacos.
5. Preheat griddle to medium heat and grill chicken for 5 minutes per side; rotating and turning as needed.
6. Remove from griddle and tent loosely with aluminum foil. Allow chicken to rest 5 minutes.
7. Serve with warm tortillas, a dollop of avocado crema, queso fresco, cilantro and lime wedges.
8. To meal prep: simply divide chicken into individual portion containers with a serving of the garnish, and take with tortillas wrapped in parchment paper to warm in a microwave to serve.

Hawaiian Chicken Skewers

Prep time: 20 minutes | Cook time: 15 minutes | Serves 4 to 5

1 pounds (454 g) boneless, skinless chicken breast, cut into 1 ½ inch cubes

3 cups pineapple, cut into 1 ½ inch cubes

2 large green pep- pers, cut into 1 ½ inch pieces

1 large red onion, cut into 1 ½ inch pieces

2 tablespoons olive oil, to coat veggies

For Marinade:

⅓ cup tomato paste

⅓ cup brown sugar, packed

⅓ cup soy sauce

¼ cup pineapple juice

2 tablespoons olive oil

1½ tablespoon mirin or rice wine vinegar

4 teaspoons garlic cloves, minced

1 tablespoon ginger, minced

½ teaspoon sesame oil

Pinch of sea salt

Pinch of ground black pepper

10 wooden skewers, for assembly

1. Combine marinade ingredients in a mixing bowl until smooth. Reserve a ½ cup of the marinade in the refrigerator.
2. Add chicken and remaining marinade to a sealable plastic bag and refrigerate for 1 hour.
3. Soak 10 wooden skewer sticks in water for 1 hour.
4. Preheat the griddle to medium heat.
5. Add red onion, bell pepper and pineapple to a mixing bowl with 2 tablespoons olive oil and toss to coat.
6. Thread red onion, bell pepper, pineapple and chicken onto the skewers until all of the chicken has been used.
7. Place skewers on griddle and grab your reserved marinade from the refrigerator; cook for 5 minutes then brush with remaining marinade and rotate.
8. Brush again with marinade and sear about 5 additional minutes or until chicken reads 165ºF (74ºC) on a meat thermometer.
9. Serve warm.

Rosemary Chicken Diavolo

Prep time: 10 minutes | Cook time: 20 minutes | Serves 4

3 pounds (1.4 kg) bone-in chicken pieces (split breasts cut in half, drumsticks, and/or thighs), trimmed
½ cup extra-virgin olive oil
4 garlic cloves, minced
1 tablespoon chopped fresh rosemary
2 teaspoons grated lemon zest plus 4 teaspoons juice
2 teaspoons red pepper flakes
1 teaspoon sugar
Salt and pepper, to taste
½ teaspoon paprika
1 cup wood chips

1. Pat chicken dry with paper towels. Whisk oil, garlic, rosemary, lemon zest, pepper flakes, sugar, 1 teaspoon pepper, and paprika together in bowl until combined. Measure out ¼ cup oil mixture and set aside for sauce. (Oil mixture can be covered and refrigerated for up to 24 hours.) Whisk 2¼ teaspoons salt into oil mixture remaining in bowl and transfer to 1-gallon zipper-lock bag. Add chicken, turn to coat, and refrigerate for at least 1 hour or up to 24 hours. Just before grilling, soak wood chips in water for 15 minutes, then drain. Using large piece of heavy-duty aluminum foil, wrap soaked chips in 8 by 4½-inch foil packet. (Make sure chips do not poke holes in sides or bottom of packet.) Cut 2 evenly spaced 2-inch slits in top of packet.
2. Preheat griddle to medium-high heat and brush with oil.
3. Remove chicken from marinade and pat dry with paper towels. Discard used marinade. Place chicken on griddle, skin side up. Cover and cook. until underside of chicken is lightly browned, 8 to 12 minutes. Flip chicken, cover, and cook until breasts register 155°F (68°C) and drumsticks/thighs register 170°F (77°C), 7 to 10 minutes.
4. Turn the griddle on high heat, skin side down, and cook until skin is well browned, about 3 minutes. Flip and continue to cook until breasts register 160°F (71°C) and drumsticks/thighs register 175°F (79°C), 1 to 3 minutes. Transfer chicken to platter, tent with foil, and let rest for 5 to 10 minutes.
5. Meanwhile, heat reserved oil mixture in small saucepan over low heat until fragrant and garlic begins to brown, 3 to 5 minutes. Off heat, whisk in lemon juice and ¼ teaspoon salt. Spoon sauce over chicken. Serve.

Chicken with Cayenne Pepper

Prep time: 10 minutes | Cook time: 45 minutes | Serves 4 to 6

1 teaspoon salt
1 teaspoon pepper
¼ teaspoon cayenne pepper
3 pounds (1.4 kg) bone-in chicken pieces (split breasts cut in half, drumsticks, and/or thighs), trimmed
1 Kansas City Barbecue Sauce

1. Combine salt, pepper, and cayenne in bowl. Pat chicken dry with paper towels and rub with spices. Reserve 2 cups barbecue sauce for cooking; set aside remaining 1 cup sauce for serving.
2. Preheat griddle to medium-high heat and brush with oil.
3. Place chicken, skin side down, on griddle. Cover and cook until chicken begins to brown, 30 to 35 minutes.
4. Cook, flipping chicken and brushing every 5 minutes with some of sauce reserved for cooking, until sticky, about 20 minutes.
5. Flipping and brushing with remaining sauce for cooking, until well glazed, breasts register 160°F (71°C), and drumsticks/thighs register 175°F (79°C), about 5 minutes. Transfer chicken to platter, tent with aluminum foil, and let rest for 5 to 10 minutes. Serve with remaining sauce.

Chicken Legs with Lime

Prep time: 12 minutes | Cook time: 20 minutes | Serves 4

2 teaspoons plus ¼ cup extra-virgin olive oil
6 garlic cloves, minced
4 teaspoons kosher salt
1 tablespoon sugar
2 teaspoons grated lime zest plus 2 table-spoons juice
1½ teaspoons ground

cumin
1 teaspoon pepper
½ teaspoon cayenne pepper
4 (10-ounce / 283-g) chicken leg quarters, trimmed
2 tablespoons chopped fresh cilantro
2 teaspoons chopped fresh oregano

1. Combine 2 teaspoons oil, garlic, salt, sugar, lime zest, cumin, pepper, and cayenne in bowl and mix to form paste. Set aside 2 teaspoons garlic paste for dressing.
2. Position chicken skin side up on cutting board and pat dry with paper towels. Leaving drumsticks and thighs attached, make 4 parallel diagonal slashes in chicken: one across drumsticks, one across leg joints; and two across thighs (each slash should reach bone). Flip chicken over and make 1 more diagonal slash across back of drumsticks. Rub remaining garlic paste all over chicken and into slashes. Refrigerate chicken for at least 1 hour or up to 24 hours.
3. Preheat griddle to medium-high heat and brush with oil.
4. Place chicken on griddle, skin side up. Cover and cook until underside of chicken is lightly browned, 9 to 12 minutes. Flip chicken, cover, and cook until leg joint registers 165ºF (74ºC), 7 to 10 minutes.
5. Turn the griddle on high heat, skin side down, and cook until skin is well browned, 3 to 5 minutes. Flip chicken and continue to cook until leg joint registers 175ºF (79ºC), about 3 minutes longer. Transfer to platter, tent with aluminum foil, and let rest for 5 to 10 minutes.
6. Meanwhile, whisk remaining ¼ cup oil, lime juice, cilantro, oregano, and reserved garlic paste together in bowl. Spoon half of dressing over chicken and serve, passing remaining dressing separately.

Fiery Italian Chicken Skewers

Prep time: 20 minutes | Cook time: 20 minutes | Serves 2-4

10 boneless, skinless chicken thighs, cut into chunks
1 large red onion, cut
For the Marinade:
¹/₃ cup toasted pine nuts
1½ cups sliced roasted red peppers
5 hot cherry peppers, stemmed and seeded, or to taste
1 cup packed fresh

into wedges
1 large red pepper, stemmed, seeded, and cut into chunks

basil leaves, plus more to serve
4 cloves garlic, peeled
¼ cup grated Parmesan cheese
1 tablespoon paprika
Extra virgin olive oil, as needed

1. Combine the toasted pine nuts, roasted red peppers, hot cherry peppers, basil, garlic, Parmesan, and paprika in a food processor or blender and process until well-combined.
2. Add in olive oil until the pesto reaches a thin consistency in order to coat the chicken as a marinade.
3. Transfer half of the pesto to a large sealable plastic bag, and reserve the other half for serving.
4. Add the chicken thigh chunks to the bag of pesto, seal, and massage the bag to coat the chicken.
5. Refrigerate for 1 hour.
6. Preheat griddle to medium-high heat and brush with olive oil.
7. Thread the chicken cubes, red onion, and red pepper onto metal skewers.
8. Brush the chicken with the reserved pesto.
9. Cook until the chicken reaches an internal temperature of 165ºF (74ºC); about 5 minutes per side. Serve warm with your favorite salad or vegetables

Chapter 4 Pork

Pork Loin with Chile

Prep time: 20 minutes | Cook time: 45 minutes | Serves 8

For the Chile de Árbol Jam:

2 ripe pineapples, peeled but left whole
2 red onions, peeled, quartered, and thinly sliced
8 chiles de árbol
2 cups sugar, plus more if needed
4 cups vinegar
1 tablespoon salt, plus more if needed
Salt, for coating
1 boneless pork loin roast (about 3 pounds / 1.4 kg)

1. Preheat griddle to medium-high heat and brush with oil.
2. To make the jam: Dice the pineapples into small pieces (about ¼ inch), including the cores, and add to a large stockpot with the onions, chiles, sugar, vinegar, and salt. Place over medium heat and let the mixture simmer, stirring occasionally but more often toward the end of cooking, until the mixture reduces and becomes sticky and jamlike, 45 minutes to 1 hour. Season with more salt and sugar, if needed. The jam can be stored in a covered container in the refrigerator for up to 2 weeks; bring to room temperature before serving.
3. Rub salt all over the pork roast and let it sit, uncovered, in the fridge for at least 4 hours and up to 24 hours. Remove the roast from the fridge an hour before you start grilling. Place it over high heat and brown all sides of the meat, 5 to 10 minutes per side. Move to medium heat and cook, turning occasionally, until an instant-read meat thermometer, placed in the thickest part of the roast, reads 145ºF (63ºC) (start checking the temperature after 45 minutes). Transfer to a cutting board and let the roast rest for 20 minutes before slicing into serving pieces. Serve with the jam.

Pork with Fish Sauce

Prep time: 30 minutes | Cook time: 8 minutes | Serves 6 to 8

1 (5-pound / 2.3-kg) Boston Butt pork shoulder

For the Marinade:

2 tablespoons garlic, minced
1 large piece ginger, peeled and chopped
1 cup hoisin sauce
¾ cup fish sauce
⅔ cup honey
⅔ cup Shaoxing
½ cup chili oil
⅓ cup oyster sauce
⅓ cup sesame oil

For the Glaze:

¾ cup dark brown sugar
1 tablespoon light molasses

1. Place pork shoulder, fat side down, on a cutting board with a short end facing you. Holding a long sharp knife about 1"–1½" above cutting board, make a shallow cut along the entire length of a long side of shoulder.
2. Continue cutting deeper into meat, lifting and unfurling with your free hand, until it lies flat.
3. Purée marinade in a blender and reserve 1 ½ cups for glaze, cover and refrigerate.
4. Pour remaining marinade in a large sealable plastic bag.
5. Add pork shoulder to bag and marinate in the refrigerator for 8 hours.
6. Preheat griddle to medium heat (with cover closed, thermometer should register 350°). Remove pork from marinade, letting excess drip off.
7. Add glaze ingredients to reserved marinade until sugar is dissolved.
8. Grill pork, for 8 minutes, basting and turning with tongs every minute or so, until thick coated with glaze, lightly charred in spots, and warmed through; an instant-read thermometer inserted into the thickest part should register 145°F (63°C).
9. Transfer to a cutting board and slice against the grain, ¼" thick, to serve.

Pork Chops with Butter

Prep time: 13 minutes | Cook time: 30 minutes | Serves 4

Salt and pepper, to taste
4 (12-ounce / 340-g) bone-in pork rib or center-cut chops, 1½ inches thick, trimmed
2 tablespoons unsalt-ed butter, softened
1 teaspoon minced fresh chives
½ teaspoon Dijon mustard
½ teaspoon grated lemon zest

1. Dissolve 3 tablespoons salt in 1½ quarts cold water in large container. Submerge pork in brine, cover, and refrigerate for 1 hour. Remove pork from brine, pat dry with paper towels, and cut slits about 2 inches apart through fat around each chop. Season with pepper. Mix butter, chives, mustard, and lemon zest in bowl and refrigerate until firm, about 15 minutes. (Chive butter can be refrigerated, covered, for up to 24 hours.)
2. Preheat griddle to medium-high heat.
3. Place chops on griddle. Cook, until browned, about 3 minutes per side. Slide chops to griddle and cook until meat registers 145°F (63°C), 7 to 9 minutes, flipping halfway through grilling. Transfer chops to platter and top with chilled chive butter. Tent with aluminum foil and let rest for 5 to 10 minutes. Serve.

Honey Pork Chops

Prep time: 20 minutes | Cook time: 35 minutes | Serves 4

4 (10-ounce / 283-g) bone-in pork rib or center-cut chops, 1 inch thick, trimmed
¼ cup sugar
1 teaspoon salt
1 teaspoon pepper
2 tablespoons cider vinegar
½ teaspoon cornstarch
¼ cup honey
1½ tablespoons Dijon mustard
½ teaspoon minced fresh thyme
⅛ teaspoon cayenne pepper

1. Pat chops dry with paper towels and cut 2 slits about 2 inches apart through fat on edges of each chop. Combine sugar, salt, and pepper in bowl, then rub thoroughly over chops.
2. Whisk vinegar and cornstarch together in small saucepan until smooth, then stir in honey, mustard, thyme, and cayenne. Bring mixture to boil, then reduce heat to medium-low and simmer until thickened and measures ¼ cup, 5 to 7 minutes.
3. Preheat griddle to medium-low heat.
4. Cook, turning as needed, until meat registers 145°F (63°C), 6 to 10 minutes.
5. Brush tops of chops with glaze, flip glazed side down, and grill over hotter part of grill until caramelized, about 1 minute. Repeat with second side of chops. Transfer chops to platter, tent with aluminum foil, and let rest for 5 to 10 minutes. Brush chops with remaining glaze before serving.

Pineapple and Bacon Pork Chops

Prep time: 30 minutes | Cook time: 1 hour | Serves 6

1 large whole pineapple
6 pork chops
For the Glaze:
¼ cup honey
⅛ teaspoon cayenne
12 slices thick-cut bacon

pepper

1. Preheat griddle to medium-high heat.
2. Slice off the top and bottom of the pineapple, and peel the pineapple, cutting the skin off in strips.
3. Cut pineapple flesh into six quarters.
4. Wrap each pineapple section with a bacon slice; secure each end with a toothpick.
5. Brush quarters with honey and sprinkle with cayenne pepper.
6. Put the quarters on the griddle, flipping when bacon is cooked so that both sides are evenly grilled.
7. While pineapple quarters are cooking, coat pork chops with honey and cayenne pepper. Set on griddle.
8. Tent with foil and cook for 20 minutes. Flip, and continue cooking an additional 10 to 20 minutes or until chops are fully cooked.
9. Serve each chop with a pineapple quarter on the side.

Pork Chops with Honey

Prep time: 25 minutes | Cook time: 25 minutes | Serves 6

6 (4-ounce / 113-g) boneless pork chops
¼ cup organic honey
1 to 2 tablespoons
low sodium soy sauce
2 tablespoons olive oil
1 tablespoon rice mirin

1. Combine honey, soy sauce, oil, and white vinegar and whisk until well-combined. Add sauce and pork chops to a large sealable plastic bag and marinate for 1 hour.
2. Preheat the griddle to medium-high heat and cook for 4 to 5 minutes, or until the pork chop easily releases from the griddle.
3. Flip and continue to cook for 5 additional minutes, or until internal temperature reaches 145°F (63°C).
4. Serve and enjoy!

Pork Chops with Paprika

Prep time: 10 minutes | Cook time: 15 minutes | Serves 4

4 pork chops
1 tablespoon paprika
½ teaspoon ground cumin
½ teaspoon dried sage
½ teaspoon salt
½ teaspoon black
pepper
½ teaspoon garlic powder
¼ teaspoon cayenne pepper
1 tablespoon butter
1 tablespoon vegetable oil

1. In a medium bowl, combine the paprika, cumin, sage, salt, pepper, garlic, and cayenne pepper.
2. Heat your griddle to medium-high heat and add the butter and oil.
3. Rub the pork chops with a generous amount of the seasoning rub.
4. Place the chops on the griddle and cook for 4 to 5 minutes. Turn the pork chops and continue cooking an additional 4 minutes.
5. Remove the pork chops from the griddle and allow to rest 5 minutes before serving.

Pork Chops with Apple

Prep time: 5 minutes | Cook time: 20 minutes | Serves 4

4, bone-in pork chops
2 honeycrisp apples, peeled, cored and chopped
⅓ cup orange juice
1 teaspoon chopped
fresh rosemary
1 teaspoon chopped fresh sage
Sea salt and black pepper, to taste

1. Add the apples, herbs and orange juice to a saucepan and simmer over medium heat until the apples are tender and the juices are thickened to a thin syrup, about 10 to 12 minutes.
2. Season pork chops with salt and pepper.
3. Place on the griddle and cook until the pork chop releases from the griddle, about 4 minutes.
4. Flip and cook on the other side for 3 minutes.
5. Transfer to a cutting board and tent with foil.
6. Top with apple compote and serve!

Pork Ribs with Ketchup

Prep time: 10 minutes | Cook time: 4 hours | Serves 6

3 pounds (1.4 kg) country-style pork ribs
1 cup low-sugar ketchup
½ cup water
¼ cup onion, finely chopped
¼ cup cider vinegar
or wine vinegar
¼ cup light molasses
2 tablespoons Worcestershire sauce
2 teaspoons chili powder
2 cloves garlic, minced

1. Combine ketchup, water, onion, vinegar, molasses, Worcestershire sauce, chili powder, and garlic in a saucepan and bring to boil; reduce heat. Simmer, uncovered, for 10 to 15 minutes or until desired thickness is reached, stirring often.
2. Trim fat from ribs.
3. Preheat griddle to medium-high.
4. Place ribs, bone-side down, on griddle and cook for 1-½ to 2 hours or until tender, brushing occasionally with sauce during the last 10 minutes of cooking.
5. Serve with remaining sauce and enjoy!

Kielbasa with Jalapeño Relish

Prep time: 13 minutes | Cook time: 25 minutes | Serves 4

For the Jalapeño Relish:

12 jalapeño chiles, stemmed, halved lengthwise, and seeded	1 tablespoon honey
	2 teaspoons salt
Oil, for coating	1½ pounds (680 g) kielbasa, cut into 5-inch lengths
1 cup vinegar	

1. Preheat griddle to medium-high heat
2. To make the relish: Toss the jalapeños with the oil, place over medium heat, and grill until charred, about 2 minutes per side. Using tongs, transfer the jalapeños to a bowl, then tightly cover with plastic wrap to allow them to steam in their own heat for 15 minutes.
3. Meanwhile, mix together the vinegar, honey, and salt in a bowl until the salt dissolves. Mince the jalapeños and combine with the vinegar mixture. The relish can be stored in a covered container in the refrigerator for at least 2 weeks; cover it with a thin layer of oil to ensure freshness.
4. To cook the kielbasa, place over medium heat and cook, turning often, until it is charred and hot throughout, about 10 minutes. Serve immediately with the relish.

Pork Chops with Sauce

Prep time: 13 minutes | Cook time: 40 minutes | Serves 4

For the Peanut–Honey Mustard Sauce:

1 cup natural-style peanut butter	peeled
	2 garlic cloves, minced
¼ cup vinegar	
2 tablespoons honey	Salt, for seasoning
2 tablespoons Pickled Mustard Seeds	4 (12- to 16-ounce / 340- to 454-g) bone-in pork rib chops, 1½ inches thick
1 teaspoon ground turmeric or 1 small knob fresh turmeric,	Salt, for coating

1. Preheat griddle to medium-high heat and brush with oil.

2. Combine the peanut butter, vinegar, honey, mustard seeds, turmeric, and garlic in a food processor. Puree until smooth, then season with salt. Set aside. The sauce can be made in advance and stored, covered, in the refrigerator for up to 2 weeks.
3. Score the fatty edge of each pork chop by cutting shallow crosshatched slices into it; this helps keep it from curling up as it cooks. Salt the chops well and let them sit for 30 minutes. Place over high heat for about 3 minutes per side. Using tongs, sear the fatty edges until the fat browns and crisps. Move to medium heat and grill, turning occasionally, for about 10 minutes more, until an instant-read meat thermometer placed in the thickest part of a chop reads 145°F (63°C). Transfer to a serving dish and let the pork rest for 10 minutes before serving with the peanut sauce.

Tangy Pork Chops

Prep time: 30 minutes | Cook time: 13 minutes | Serves 4

4 (½-inch-thick) bone-in pork chops	Kosher salt and freshly ground black pepper, to taste
3 tablespoons olive oil, plus more for grill	
For the Marinade:	
1 habanero chili, seeded, chopped fine	juice
2 garlic cloves, minced	2 tablespoons brown sugar
½ cup fresh orange	1 tablespoon apple cider vinegar

1. Combine marinade ingredients in a large sealable plastic bag.
2. Pierce pork chops all over with a fork and add to bag, seal, and turn to coat.
3. Marinate at room temperature, turning occasionally, for 30 minutes.
4. Prepare griddle for medium-high heat.
5. Brush the griddle with oil.
6. Remove pork chops from marinade and pat dry.
7. Sear for 8 minutes, turning occasionally, until charred and cooked through.
8. Transfer to a plate and let rest 5 minutes.
9. Serve with your favorite sides.

Pork Paillards with Lime

Prep time: 15 minutes | Cook time: 23 minutes | Serves 4 to 6

For the Marinade:

4 cups water	peppercorns, cracked
Juice of 2 limes (about ¼ cup)	2 pounds (907 g) thin-cut boneless
4 garlic cloves, minced	pork shoulder steaks, ¼ inch thick
¼ cup sugar	Salt, for finishing
2 tablespoons salt	Lemon or lime wedges, for serving
2 teaspoons black	

1. Preheat griddle to medium-high heat.
2. To make the marinade: Mix together the water, lime juice, garlic, sugar, salt, and peppercorns in a large bowl and let sit until the sugar and salt dissolve.
3. Add the pork to the marinade and let sit at room temperature for 1 hour or refrigerate, covered, for up to 4 hours. Just before grilling, remove the pork from the marinade and pat dry.
4. Cook the pork over high heat for 1 minute, then rotate 45 degrees and cook for another minute. Flip and repeat on the other side. Transfer to a serving platter in a high pile, sprinkle with salt, and serve with lemon wedges.

Baby Back Ribs with BBQ Sauce

Prep time: 20 minutes | Cook time: 45 minutes | Serves 4

For the Tamarind Barbecue Sauce:

1 tablespoon oil	1 cup water, plus more if needed
1 white onion, peeled and thinly sliced	2 tablespoons honey, plus more if needed
½ cup chipotle chiles, stemmed and seeded	1 teaspoon salt, plus more if needed
1 cup freshly squeezed orange juice (from 4 to 6 oranges)	4 pounds (1.8 kg) baby back ribs (ask your butcher to re-
1 cup tamarind paste	move the membrane)
8 garlic cloves, chopped	Salt and pepper, for seasoning
1 cup vinegar, plus more if needed	

1. Preheat griddle to medium-high heat and brush with oil.

2. To make the sauce: Add the onion and cook until softened and slightly caramelized, about 5 minutes. Add the chipotles and cook for another 2 minutes. Deglaze the orange juice, add the tamarind paste, garlic, vinegar, water, honey, and salt, and simmer for 20 minutes or until the liquid thickens enough to coat a spoon. Cool slightly, then transfer to a blender and blend until very smooth, adding more vinegar and/or water if needed to thin to a consistency of tomato sauce. Add more vinegar, honey, or salt, if needed. The sauce can be stored in a covered container in the refrigerator for up to 2 weeks.
3. Season the ribs with salt and pepper. Cook over medium heat, turning often, for about 45 minutes or until they're no longer pink in the middle and the meat starts to shrink away from the bones at the edges. Baste frequently with the sauce so it builds up a thick, tacky crust. Transfer to a cutting board and immediately slice the ribs into two-rib portions. Serve the ribs on a platter.

Buttery Pork Chops

Prep time: 30 minutes | Cook time: 1 hour | Serves 4 to 6

4 to 6 pork chops	½ teaspoon garlic powder
4 cloves garlic, finely chopped	½ teaspoon salt
½ cup olive oil	½ black pepper
½ cup soy sauce	¼ cup butter

1. In a large zipperlock bag, combine the garlic, olive oil, soy sauce, and garlic powder. Add the pork chops and make sure the marinade coats the chops. Set aside for 30 minutes.
2. Heat your griddle to medium-high heat. Add 2 tablespoons of olive oil and 2 tablespoons of butter to the griddle.
3. Add the chops to the griddle one at a time, making sure they are not crowded. Add another 2 tablespoons of butter to the griddle and cook the chops for 4 minutes. Cook an additional 4 minutes.
4. Remove the chops from the griddle and spread the remaining butter over them. Serve after resting for 5 minutes.

Bean and Ham Hock Soup

Prep time: 20 minutes | Cook time: 2¼ hours | Serves 4 to 6

1½ pounds (680 g) smoked ham hocks
Oil, for coating
1 white onion, minced
2 carrots, minced
2 celery stalks, minced
1 pound (454 g) dried black beans
3-inch-long piece daikon radish (optional)
4 bay leaves
1 tablespoon cumin seeds, crushed or ground
10 cups water, plus more if needed
Salt, for seasoning

1. Preheat griddle to medium-high heat and brush with oil.
2. Cook the ham hocks over high heat until deeply browned, 5 to 10 minutes per side.
3. While the ham hocks are cooking, Add the onion, carrots, and celery and cook until the onions start to brown, about 10 minutes. Add the ham hocks, beans, radish (if using), bay leaves, cumin, and water. Cook for at least 2 hours over medium heat, until the beans are very soft (they should crush easily between your fingers), adding more water if necessary to keep the beans covered. If the soup seems too thin, simmer, uncovered, to thicken, or, if it's too thick, add more water until you achieve the desired consistency.
4. Remove the ham hocks (and the daikon, if using) and, when the ham is cool enough to handle, pick the meat from the bones, discarding the bones and skin. Return the meat to the pot and season with salt. Serve immediately.

Lime Pork Chops

Prep time: 10 minutes | Cook time: 1 to 1½ hour | Serves 4

4 pork chops
4 cloves garlic, smashed
2 tablespoons olive oil
⅓ cup lime juice
¼ cup water
1 teaspoon ground cumin
Salt and black pepper, to taste

1. Set your griddle to medium. Salt the pork chops on both side and cook the chops until lightly browned.
2. Combine the water, garlic, and lime juice in a bowl and whisk until even.
3. Continue cooking the pork chops while basting them with the lime juice mixture.
4. When the pork chops have finished cooking, remove from the griddle and top with additional sauce and black pepper before serving.

Tangy Pork Tenderloins

Prep time: 15 minutes | Cook time: 8 minutes | Serves 4

2 pork tenderloins, trimmed
1 teaspoon annatto powder
Olive oil
For the Marinade:
2 oranges, juiced
2 lemons, juiced, or more to taste
2 limes, juiced, or more to taste
6 cloves garlic, minced
1 teaspoon ground
cumin
½ teaspoon cayenne pepper
½ teaspoon dried oregano
½ teaspoon black pepper

1. Combine marinade ingredients in a mixing bowl and whisk until well-blended.
2. Cut the tenderloins in half crosswise; cut each piece in half lengthwise.
3. Place pieces in marinade and thoroughly coat with the mixture.
4. Cover with plastic wrap and refrigerate 4 to 6 hours.
5. Transfer pieces of pork from marinade to a paper-towel-lined bowl to absorb most of the moisture.
6. Discard paper towels. Drizzle olive oil and a bit more annatto powder on the pork.
7. Preheat griddle for medium-high heat and lightly oil.
8. Place pieces evenly spaced on griddle; cook 4 to 5 minutes.
9. Turn and cook on the other side another 4 or 5 minutes.
10. Transfer onto a serving platter and allow meat to rest about 5 minutes before serving.

Pork Chops with Honey Vinegar

Prep time: 10 minutes | Cook time: 18 minutes | Serves 4

For the Honey Vinegar:

¼ cup honey	4 (8- to 12-ounce /
2 cups warm water	227- to 340-g) bone-
Salt and oil, for coat-	in pork rib chops, 1
ing	inch thick

1. To make the honey vinegar: Combine the honey and water in a quart jar, cover with a cloth (this will let air in but will keep fruit flies out), and secure with a rubber band. Keep in a warm place—a high shelf or a countertop that receives direct sunlight—for at least 4 weeks, or until fermented and slightly effervescent. Strain through a fine-mesh strainer or cheesecloth and store in a sealed jar in the refrigerator.
2. Preheat griddle to medium-high heat and brush with oil.
3. Salt the chops well and let them sit for 30 minutes. Add the pork chops and cook for 2 minutes per side, until deeply browned. Remove the chops to a plate. Deglaze the griddle with the honey vinegar and reduce for about 45 seconds, then return the pork chops to the pan. Continue reducing the honey vinegar and baste the pork with it, until it reduces to the consistency of maple syrup. Let the pork chops rest for 5 minutes before serving.

Glazed Pork Tenderloins

Prep time: 13 minutes | Cook time: 20 minutes | Serves 4 to 6

2 (12- to 16-ounce /	sesame oil
340- to 454-g) pork	2 garlic cloves,
tenderloins, trimmed	minced
½ cup soy sauce	1 teaspoon five-spice
½ cup apricot	powder
preserves	1 teaspoon pepper
¼ cup hoisin sauce	¼ cup ketchup
¼ cup dry sherry	1 tablespoon molas-
2 tablespoons grated	ses
fresh ginger	2 teaspoons vegeta-
1 tablespoon toasted	ble oil

1. Lay tenderloins on cutting board with long side running almost perpendicular to counter edge. Cut horizontally down length of each tenderloin, stopping ½ inch from edge so tenderloin remains intact. Working with one at a time, open up tenderloins, place between 2 sheets of plastic wrap, and pound to ¾-inch thickness.
2. Combine soy sauce, preserves, hoisin, sherry, ginger, sesame oil, garlic, five-spice powder, and pepper in bowl. Measure out ¾ cup of marinade and set aside. Place pork in large zipper-lock bag and pour remaining marinade into bag with pork. Seal bag, turn to coat, and refrigerate for at least 30 minutes or up to 4 hours.
3. Combine reserved marinade, ketchup, and molasses in small saucepan. Cook over medium heat until syrupy and reduced to ¾ cup, 3 to 5 minutes. Reserve ¼ cup glaze for glazing cooked pork.
4. Preheat griddle to medium-high heat.
5. Clean and oil your griddle. Pat pork dry with paper towels, then rub with vegetable oil. Place pork on griddle and cook until lightly charred on first side, about 2 minutes. Flip and brush grilled side of pork evenly with 2 tablespoons glaze. Continue grilling until lightly charred on second side, about 2 minutes. Flip and brush evenly with 2 tablespoons glaze. Repeat flipping and glazing twice more, until pork registers 145ºF (63ºC) and is thickly glazed, about 4 minutes longer. Transfer pork to cutting board and brush with reserved glaze. Tent with aluminum foil and let rest for 5 minutes. Slice and serve.

Chapter 5 Beef and Lamb

Basic Juicy NY Strip Steak

Prep time: 45 minutes | Cook time: 8 minutes | Serves 1

1 (8-ounce / 227-g) NY strip steak
Olive oil
Sea salt, to taste
Fresh ground black pepper, to taste

1. Remove the steak from the refrigerator and let it come to room temperature, about 30 to 45 minutes.
2. Preheat griddle to medium-high heat and brush with olive oil.
3. Season the steak on all sides with salt and pepper.
4. Cook steak about 4 to 5 minutes.
5. Flip and cook about 4 minutes more for medium rare steak; between 125°F (52°C) and 130°F (54°C) on a meat thermometer.
6. Transfer the steak to a plate and let it rest for 5 minutes before serving.

Caprese Grilled Filet Mignon

Prep time: 10 minutes | Cook time: 10 minutes | Serves 4

4 (6-ounce / 170-g) filets
1 teaspoon garlic salt
Italian Olive oil
2 roma tomatoes, sliced
4 ounces fresh buffalo mozzarella, cut into
four slices
8 fresh basil leaves
Balsamic vinegar glaze, for drizzling
Sea salt, for seasoning
Fresh ground pepper

1. Lightly brush each filet, on all sides, with olive oil and rub with garlic salt.
2. Preheat griddle to high. Place steaks on griddle, reduce heat to medium, tent with foil and cook for 5 minutes.
3. Flip, re-tent, and cook for an additional 5 minutes; during the last 2 minutes of grilling top each with a slice of Mozzarella.
4. Remove steaks from the griddle and top each with a few tomato slices, 2 basil leafs.
5. Drizzle with balsamic, sprinkle with sea salt and black pepper and serve.

Steak with Cheese

Prep time: 6 minutes | Cook time: 8 minutes | Serves 4

1 (24-ounce / 680-g) dry-aged New York strip steak
Salt and pepper, for coating
½ cup blue cheese,
such as Roquefort, Gorgonzola, Bleu d'Auvergne, or Danish Blue
2 tablespoons oil

1. Preheat griddle to medium-high heat.
2. Pat the steak dry and coat with salt and pepper. Let sit for 20 to 30 minutes. Place the steak over high heat for 5 minutes, then flip and repeat. Move to medium heat and cook for another 2 to 3 minutes, until an instant-read meat thermometer, placed in the thickest part of the steak, reads 125ºF (52ºC). Transfer to a cutting board and let rest for 10 minutes.
3. While the steak is cooling, combine the cheese and oil in a food processor and blend until smooth and fluffy, about 1 minute. Slice the steak against the grain and top with the blue cheese mixture just before serving.

Beef Steak with Salt

Prep time: 8 minutes | Cook time: 15 minutes | Serves 4

2 porterhouse steaks, about 1½ inches thick
Butcher's salt , for coating

1. Preheat griddle to medium-high heat.
2. Pat the steaks dry and coat with the salt. Let sit for 20 to 30 minutes. Place the steaks over high heat. Cook for about 2 minutes, then turn the steaks 45 degrees and cook for another 2 minutes. Flip and repeat on the other side. Cook, flipping occasionally, until an instant-read meat thermometer, placed in the thickest part of one steak, reads 125ºF (52ºC) (this shouldn't take much longer than 8 to 10 minutes total). Transfer to a cutting board and let rest for 10 minutes before slicing and serving.

Strip Steak with Pepper

Prep time: 45 minutes | Cook time: 8 minutes | Serves 1

1 (8-ounce / 227-g) NY strip steak
Olive oil

Sea salt and fresh ground black pepper, to taste

1. Remove the steak from the refrigerator and let it come to room temperature, about 30 to 45 minutes.
2. Preheat griddle to medium-high heat and brush with olive oil.
3. Season the steak on all sides with salt and pepper.
4. Cook steak about 4 to 5 minutes.
5. Flip and cook about 4 minutes more for medium rare steak; between 125ºF (52ºC) and 130ºF (54ºC) on a meat thermometer.
6. Transfer the steak to a plate and let it rest for 5 minutes before serving.

Strip Steak with Sage

Prep time: 23 minutes | Cook time: 15 minutes | Serves 2

2 (1-pound / 454-g) New York strip steaks,
For the Rub:
1 bunch thyme sprigs
1 bunch rosemary sprigs
1 bunch sage sprigs
1½ teaspoons black pepper, divided
¾ teaspoon sea salt, divided

trimmed

½ teaspoon garlic powder
2 tablespoons chopped fresh flat-leaf parsley
2 tablespoons extra-virgin olive oil

1. Preheat griddle to high heat.
2. Combine rub ingredients in a small mixing bowl and rub steaks with spice mixture; let rest 10 minutes.
3. Place steaks on griddle and cook 1 minute per side.
4. Turn griddle down to medium heat.
5. Turn steaks and grill 3 additional minutes per side; or until thermometer registers 135°F for medium rare.
6. Remove steaks to a platter.
7. Let rest 5 minutes. Cut steaks across grain into thin slices.

Beef Steaks with Zucchini

Prep time: 10 minutes | Cook time: 15 minutes | Serves 6

For the Steak:
2 (1-pound / 454-g) sirloin steaks
1 tablespoon garlic powder
4 tablespoons soy sauce
1 white onion, sliced into large rounds

3 zucchini, sliced into ¼ inch thick flats
2 cups snap peas
4 tablespoons vegetable oil
3 tablespoons butter
Salt and black pepper, to taste

1. Season the steak with salt, pepper, and garlic powder.
2. Set your griddle to high heat on one side and medium-high heat on the other side.
3. Add some vegetable oil to the medium-hot side and add the onion rings, zucchini, and snap peas. Season with a little salt and pepper.
4. Add the steaks to the hot side and cook for 3 minutes. Flip, top with butter and add soy sauce to the steaks. Continue cooking an additional 4 minutes.
5. Remove the steak and vegetables from the griddle and slice the steak across the grain before serving.

Lamb Shoulder Chops

Prep time: 8 minutes | Cook time: 20 minutes | Serves 4

4 (8- to 12-ounce / 227- to 340-g) lamb shoulder chops (blade or round bone), ¾ to 1 inch thick, trimmed

2 tablespoons extra-virgin olive oil
Salt and pepper, to taste

1. Preheat griddle to medium-high heat and brush with olive oil, about 15 minutes.
2. Rub chops with oil and season with salt and pepper. Place chops on griddle and cook until well browned, about 2 minutes per side. Slide chops to griddle and continue to cook until meat registers 120ºF (49ºC) to 125ºF (52ºC) (for medium-rare) or 130ºF (54ºC) to 135ºF (57ºC) (for medium), 2 to 4 minutes per side. Transfer chops to large platter, tent with aluminum foil, and let rest for 5 minutes before serving.

High-Low Strip Steak

Prep time: 10 minutes | Cook time: 15 minutes | Serves 2

2 (1-pound / 454-g) New York strip steaks, trimmed

For the Rub:

1 bunch thyme sprigs	½ teaspoon garlic powder
1 bunch rosemary sprigs	2 tablespoons chopped fresh flat-leaf parsley
1 bunch sage sprigs	
1½ teaspoons black pepper, divided	2 tablespoons extra-virgin olive oil
¾ teaspoon sea salt, divided	

1. Preheat griddle to high heat.
2. Combine rub ingredients in a small mixing bowl and rub steaks with spice mixture; let rest 10 minutes.
3. Place steaks on griddle and cook 1 minute per side.
4. Turn griddle down to medium heat.
5. Turn steaks and grill 3 additional minutes per side; or until thermometer registers 135°F (57°C) for medium rare.
6. Remove steaks to a platter.
7. Let rest 5 minutes. Cut steaks across grain into thin slices

Tuscan-Style Steak with Crispy Potatoes

Prep time: 30 minutes | Cook time: 35 minutes | Serves 4

2 bone-in porterhouse steaks	taste
1½ pounds (680 g) small potatoes, like Yukon Gold, scrubbed but skins left on, halved	2 teaspoons red wine, like Sangiovese or Montepulciano
	1 teaspoon balsamic vinegar
4 tablespoons extra-virgin olive oil, divided	Pinch red pepper flakes
Sea salt and freshly ground pepper, to	3 fresh rosemary sprigs, needles removed (discard stems)

1. Add potatoes to a large pot and cover with water, bring to a boil over high heat, then reduce the heat to medium-high and cook until the potatoes are almost tender, about 10 minutes. Drain, add to a medium mixing bowl, coat with 2 tablespoons olive oil, and set aside.
2. Preheat griddle to medium heat.
3. Whisk 2 tablespoons olive oil, rosemary, red wine, vinegar, and pepper flakes; add steaks to marinade and set aside until ready to cook.
4. Sprinkle potatoes with salt and pepper.
5. Add steaks to one side of the griddle and potatoes to the other.
6. Cook steak for 5 minutes, flip and 4 minutes on the other side for medium rare.
7. Add the potatoes to cook for 5 minutes.
8. Transfer steaks to a cutting board and tent with aluminum foil and let rest for 5 minutes while potatoes are cooking.
9. Divide each steak into 2 pieces and divide among 4 dinner plates. Spoon some potatoes around the steak and serve hot!

Teppanyaki Beef With Vegetable

Prep time: 10 minutes | Cook time: 15 minutes | Serves 6

For the Steak:

2 (1-pound / 454-g) sirloin steaks	3 zucchini, sliced into ¼ inch thick flats
1 tablespoon garlic powder	2 cups snap peas
4 tablespoons soy sauce	4 tablespoons vegetable oil
1 white onion, sliced into large rounds	3 tablespoons butter
	Salt and black pepper, to taste

1. Season the steak with salt, pepper, and garlic powder.
2. Set your griddle to high heat on one side and medium-high heat on the other side.
3. Add some vegetable oil to the medium-hot side and add the onion rings, zucchini, and snap peas. Season with a little salt and pepper.
4. Add the steaks to the hot side and cook for 3 minutes. Flip, top with butter and add soy sauce to the steaks. Continue cooking an additional 4 minutes.
5. Remove the steak and vegetables from the griddle and slice the steak across the grain before serving

Rib-Eye Steak with Herbed Steak Butter

Prep time: 12 minutes | Cook time: 50 minutes | Serves 2-4

1 (24-ounce / 680-g) bone-in Tomahawk rib-eye, about 2 ½ inches thick Olive oil Sea salt, to taste	Fresh cracked pepper, to taste 3 tablespoons premium French butter ½ teaspoon Herbed de Provence

1. Beat butter with herbs in a small mixing bowl, cover and refrigerate until ready to grill rib-eye.
2. Rub the rib-eye liberally with olive oil, salt and pepper until entire steak is covered.
3. Wrap lightly with cling wrap and place in the refrigerator to marinate for 12 hours.
4. Preheat the griddle to high heat on one side and medium low on the other side, at least one hour prior to cooking.
5. Remove the steak from the refrigerator and leave at room temperature during the hour that the griddle is preheating.
6. Place the steak on the center of the hottest side of the griddle. Do this for both sides, about 10 minutes.
7. Move the rib-eye to the cooler side of the griddle and cook to rare, about 25 to 30 minutes.
8. Transfer rib-eye to a grill rack, add herbed butter on top, and lightly tent it with tin foil to rest for at least 15 minutes before carving.
9. Serve with your favorite sides

Texas-Style Brisket

Prep time: 10 minutes | Cook time: 6 hours 20 minutes | Serves 6

1 (4½-pound / 2.0-kg) flat cut beef bris- **For the Rub:** 1 tablespoon sea salt 1 tablespoon dark brown sugar 2 teaspoons smoked paprika 2 teaspoons chili powder 1 teaspoon garlic	ket (about 3 inches thick) powder 1 teaspoon onion powder 1 teaspoon ground black pepper 1 teaspoon mesquite liquid smoke, like Colgin

1. Combine the rub ingredients in a small mixing bowl.
2. Rinse and pat brisket dry and rub with coffee mix.
3. Preheat the griddle for two zone cooking; heat one side to high and leaving one side with low heat.
4. Sear on high heat side for 3 to 5 minutes on each side or until nicely charred.
5. Move to low heat side, tent with foil, and cook for 6 hours or until a meat thermometer registers 195°F (91°C).
6. Remove from griddle. Let stand, covered, 30 minutes.
7. Cut brisket across grain into thin slices and serve

Tender Steak with Pineapple Rice

Prep time: 10 minutes | Cook time: 10 minutes | Serves 4

4 (4-ounce / 113-g) beef fillets ¼ cup soy sauce ½ teaspoon black pepper ½ teaspoon garlic powder 1 (8-ounce / 227-g) can pineapple chunks,	in juice, drained 2 scallions, thin sliced 2 (9-ounce / 255-g) packages pre-cooked brown rice, like Uncle Ben's 1 teaspoon kosher salt Olive oil, for brushing

1. Combine soy sauce, pepper, garlic powder, and beef in a large sealable plastic bag.
2. Seal and massage sauce into beef; let stand at room temperature for 7 minutes, turning bag occasionally.
3. Preheat griddle to medium-high heat and brush with olive oil.
4. Add pineapple and green onions to grill and cook 5 minutes or until well charred, turning to char evenly.
5. Remove pineapple mix and brush with additional olive oil.
6. Add steaks and cook 3 minutes on each side, for rare, or until desired temperature is reached.
7. Cook rice according to package instructions.
8. Add rice, pineapple, onions, and salt to a bowl and stir gently to combine.
9. Plate steaks with pineapple rice and serve!

Caprese Flank Steak

Prep time: 10 minutes | Cook time: 10 minutes | Serves 4

4 (6-ounce / 170-g) flank steaks	2 Roma tomatoes, sliced
Sea salt, for seasoning	4 ounces (113 g) fresh buffalo mozzarella, cut into four slices
Flakey sea salt, for serving	8 fresh basil leaves
Fresh ground pepper, to taste	Balsamic vinegar glaze, for drizzling
Olive oil	

1. Lightly brush each filet, on all sides, with olive oil and season with salt and pepper.
2. Preheat griddle to high. Place steaks on griddle, reduce heat to medium, tent with foil and cook for 5 minutes.
3. Flip, re-tent, and cook for an additional 5 minutes; during the last 2 minutes of cooking, top each with a slice of mozzarella.
4. Remove steaks from the griddle and top each with a few tomato slices, 2 basil leafs.
5. Drizzle with balsamic glaze, and sprinkle with flakey salt and a little more black pepper.

Flank Steak with Garlic and Rosemary

Prep time: 10 minutes | Cook time: 20 minutes | Serves 4

2 (8-ounce / 227-g)	flank steaks

For the Marinade:

1 tablespoon extra virgin olive oil, plus more for brushing	4 cloves garlic, minced
2 tablespoons fresh rosemary, chopped	2 teaspoons sea salt
	¼ teaspoon black pepper

1. Add marinade ingredients to a food processor or blender and pulse until garlic and rosemary are pulverized.
2. Use a fork to pierce the steaks 10 times on each side.
3. Rub each evenly with the marinade on both sides.
4. Place in a covered dish and refrigerate for at least 1 hour or overnight.

5. Preheat griddle to high and brush with olive oil and preheat to high.
6. Cook steaks for 5 minutes, flip, tent with foil, and cook for about 3-4 minutes more.
7. Transfer meat to rest on a cutting board, cover with aluminum foil, for about 15 minutes.
8. Slice very thin against the grain and serve immediately

Lamb Chops with BBQ Sauce

Prep time: 15 minutes | Cook time: 35 minutes | Serves 4

For the Tomatillo Barbecue Sauce:

10 large tomatillos, peeled and rinsed	2½ pounds (1.1 kg) lamb ribs or loin chops, each at least 1 inch thick
5 jalapeño chiles	
2 cups vinegar	
2 cups water	Salt, for seasoning
¾ cup sugar	
1 tablespoon salt	

1. Preheat griddle to medium-high heat.
2. To make the sauce: Place the tomatillos and jalapeños over medium heat, turning occasionally, until slightly charred all over, about 8 minutes total. Transfer to a plate and cut the tomatillos in half, reserving the juice. Halve the jalapeños lengthwise, remove the stems, and scrape out some of the seeds and veins. Combine the tomatillos (with their juice) and jalapeños together with the vinegar, water, sugar, and salt in a medium saucepan and simmer over low heat for 20 to 30 minutes, until the sauce is reduced and slightly syrupy. Cool the mixture slightly, transfer to a blender, and blend until very smooth. The sauce can be covered and refrigerated for up to 1 week.
3. Salt the chops well, then place them over high heat and sear on all sides (use tongs to crisp up the fat on the edges), about 2 minutes per side. Move to medium heat and cook, turning often, until just past medium-rare (about 135ºF (57ºC) on an instant-read meat thermometer), about 5 minutes more in total. Transfer to a serving platter and let rest for 5 minutes before serving, passing the sauce separately.

Rib Eye Steak with Butter

Prep time: 10 minutes | Cook time: 30 minutes | Serves 1

1 unpeeled white or red onion Oil, for coating 1 tablespoon molasses (may substitute honey) 1 tablespoon butter	Salt, for seasoning and coating 1 (1-pound / 454-g) bone-in rib eye steak, about 1½ inches thick Pepper, for coating

1. Preheat griddle to medium-high heat and brush with oil.
2. Roast the onion directly onto the griddle until it feels soft when prodded with tongs, about 20 minutes. Transfer to a cutting board, remove skin, and chop the flesh finely. Add the onion and cook until it's deep brown. Add the molasses and cook for another 5 minutes, then add the butter, season with salt, and keep the sauce warm on a corner of the grill while you cook the rib eye.
3. Coat the steak generously with salt and pepper and let sit for 20 to 30 minutes. Preheat griddle to high heat and sear for about 6 minutes per side, turning often, until it's deeply browned. Remove from heat when an instant-read meat thermometer, placed in the thickest part, reads 130ºF (54ºC). Transfer to a serving plate and let sit for 10 minutes before eating with the caramelized onions.

Filet Mignon with Herb Mayo

Prep time: 6 minutes | Cook time: 10 minutes | Serves 4

4 (8-ounce / 227-g) filet mignon steaks, 2 inches thick **For the Herb Mayo:** ½ cup minced mixed fresh herbs, such as parsley, basil, and mint 2 tablespoons minced fennel fronds (may	Salt and pepper, for coating ½ cup (1 stick) butter substitute minced tarragon leaves) 1 teaspoon lemon zest 1 cup mayonnaise Salt, for seasoning

1. Preheat griddle to medium-high heat.

2. Coat the steaks generously with salt and pepper. Heat griddle over high heat. Add the butter, and when it starts to smell nutty and turn color, add the steaks and turn them in the butter to coat. Sear on all sides until a dark crust forms, 2 to 3 minutes per side. Transfer to the grill over medium heat and let cook, turning often, until an instant-read meat thermometer, placed in the thickest part of one steak, reads 125ºF (52ºC). Transfer to a platter and let the steaks rest for 10 minutes before serving.
3. While the meat is cooking, make the mayo: In a small bowl, mix the herbs, fennel, and lemon zest into the mayonnaise and season with salt. Serve the steaks with the mayo on the side.

Lamb Legs

Prep time: 15 minutes | Cook time: 1 hour | Serves 8 to 10

1 (3½- to 4-pound / 1.59- to 1.8-kg) boneless half leg of lamb, trimmed	2 tablespoons vegetable oil Salt and pepper, to taste

1. Cover lamb with plastic wrap and pound to even thickness as needed. Let stand at room temperature, covered loosely with plastic, for 1 hour.
2. Preheat griddle to medium-high heat and brush with olive oil.
3. Meanwhile, pat lamb dry with paper towels, then rub with oil and season with salt and pepper.
4. Place lamb fat side down on griddle. Cook until well browned, about 10 minutes, rotating meat halfway through grilling so that meat facing hotter side is now facing cooler side.
5. Flip lamb fat side up and continue to cook on griddle, covered, for 5 minutes. Rotate meat and move to griddle (if using charcoal); , cook until meat registers 120ºF (49ºC) to 125ºF (52ºC) (for medium-rare) or 130ºF (54ºC) to 135ºF (57ºC) (for medium), 5 to 15 minutes.
6. Transfer lamb to carving board, tent with aluminum foil, and let rest for 20 minutes. Slice thin on bias and serve.

Greek Flank Steak Gyros

Prep time: 5 minutes | Cook time: 20 minutes | Serves 4

1 pound (454 g) flank steak
1 white onion, thinly sliced
1 roma tomato, thinly sliced

1 cucumber, peeled and thinly sliced
¼ cup crumbled feta cheese
4 6-inch pita pockets

For the Marinade:

¼ cup olive oil, plus more for brushing
1 teaspoon dried oregano
1 teaspoon balsamic vinegar

1 teaspoon garlic powder
Sea salt and freshly ground pepper, to taste

For the Sauce:

1 cup plain yogurt
2 tablespoons fresh dill (can use dried), chopped

1 teaspoon garlic, minced
2 tablespoons lemon juice

1. Cut the flank steak into thin strips against the grain. Add the marinade ingredients to a large sealable plastic bag, add the sliced meat, seal, and turn to coat.
2. Place in the refrigerator to marinate for 2 hours or overnight.
3. Preheat the griddle to medium-high heat, and an oven to 250°F.
4. Combine the sauce ingredients in small mixing bowl and set aside.
5. Spritz the pitas with a little water, wrap in foil and place in the oven to warm.
6. Brush griddle with olive oil.
7. Add meat to grill and discard marinade. Cook until brown and cooked through, about 5 minutes.
8. Remove the pitas from the oven, and cut in half.
9. Arrange the pitas on plates and stuff with cucumber, tomato, onions, and beef.
10. Spoon some yogurt sauce over the meat and top with feta and serve.

Skirt Steak with Chiles

Prep time: 13 minutes | Cook time: 30 minutes | Serves 4 to 6

For the Coriander–Ancho Rub:

2 tablespoons coriander seeds
4 ancho chiles, stemmed, seeded,

and roughly torn
2 teaspoons salt
1 tablespoon honey

For the Gribiche:

4 hard-boiled eggs, peeled and minced
2 tablespoons minced parsley leaves
2 tablespoons minced shallots
Zest and juice of 1 lemon (about 3 table-

spoons juice)
½ cup oil
Salt and pepper, for seasoning
2 pounds (907 g) skirt steak (ask your butcher for "outside skirt")

1. To make the rub: Place the coriander and chiles in a skillet over medium heat and stir until toasted and fragrant but not burnt, 3 to 5 minutes. Cool slightly and blend to a fine powder in a blender or food processor. Mix with the salt and honey. The rub will keep tightly covered in the refrigerator for up to 2 weeks.
2. To make the gribiche: Combine the eggs, parsley, shallots, and lemon zest and juice in a bowl. Slowly add the oil, while whisking constantly. Season with salt and pepper. Gribiche can be covered and refrigerated for up to 8 hours, but should be served on the day it's made.
3. Coat the steaks liberally with the rub. Let them rest uncovered in the refrigerator for at least 1 hour and up to 4 hours.
4. Preheat griddle to high
5. Place the steak over high heat for about 90 seconds, then turn 45 degrees and cook for another 90 seconds. Flip and repeat on the other side, for a total of 6 minutes. Move to medium heat and test for doneness by slicing into one steak; you don't want it cooked beyond medium-rare. Transfer steak to a cutting board and let rest for 5 minutes, then slice against the grain and serve with the gribiche.

Rib Roast with Potato

Prep time: 13 minutes | Cook time: 3½ hours | Serves 6 to 8

1 (4- to 5-pound / 1.8- to 2.3-kg) standing rib roast
Salt and pepper, for seasoning
1 apple, of any variety
2 large shallots
1 large bunch mixed herbs (with stems), such as rosemary,
sage, tarragon, and parsley, tied at the base to make a "broom"
6 to 8 large russet potatoes (at least 1 per person)
¼ cup store-bought black garlic, peeled
2 cups sour cream

1. Season the roast generously with salt and pepper and let it sit, covered, at room temperature for 2 hours before cooking. This will bring the meat to room temperature all the way through, so you don't risk having cool meat at the center after cooking.
2. Meanwhile, preheat griddle to medium-high heat.
3. Place the roast bone side down over medium heat and put the apple and shallots directly onto the griddle. After about 30 minutes, start turning the roast occasionally, so that every exposed part gets deeply browned (the bone side should get the most time on the grill, since that meat takes longer to cook).
4. As the roast browns and the fat renders from the surface, brush the roast firmly with the herb broom, allowing some of the leaves to fall onto the roast. When the shallot and apple are very soft and almost falling apart, use tongs to rub them all over the roast as it cooks. You want to build up a shallot-apple-herb crust that will both flavor and protect the meat.
5. After about 1 hour, put the potatoes onto the griddle under the roast so they catch some of the drippings. No need to prick the potatoes; if any of them explode, which is unlikely, it makes a good story, and they'll absorb more of the tasty beef fat. The roast should take about 2 hours to cook through (move it to higher heat if it's not building up a deeply colored crust), but after about 90 minutes, start checking the temperature with an instant-read meat thermometer. Cook to an internal temperature of 130ºF (54ºC) (because of its ample fat marbling, rib roast is best when it's not too rare).
6. Remove the roast to a cutting board using potholder-covered hands or two large forks. Tent with aluminum foil and let it rest for 20 to 30 minutes. When the potatoes can be easily pierced with a butter knife, use tongs to remove them, wrap with foil, and let sit on a corner of the grill to keep warm.
7. While the roast is resting, mash the black garlic with a fork in a bowl until very smooth. Add the sour cream and whisk until smooth and fluffy. Using scissors, snip the herbs from the herb broom directly into the sauce.
8. Remove the potatoes from the foil and arrange them around the roast on the platter. To serve, carve the roast at the table and pass the sauce alongside.

Lamb Kebabs

Prep time: 14 minutes | Cook time: 40 minutes | Serves 6

1 marinade
2¼ pounds (1 kg) boneless leg of lamb (shank end), trimmed and cut into 1-inch pieces
3 bell peppers (1 red, 1 yellow, and 1 orange), stemmed,
seeded, and each cut into twenty-four 1-inch pieces
1 large red onion, cut into thirty-six ¾-inch pieces
Lemon or lime wedges (optional)

1. Toss marinade and lamb in 1-gallon zipper-lock plastic bag or large bowl; seal bag, pressing out as much air as possible, or cover bowl and refrigerate for at least 2 hours or up to 24 hours.
2. Starting and ending with meat, thread 4 pieces meat, 3 pieces onion (three 3-layer stacks), and 6 pieces bell pepper in mixed order on each of 12 metal skewers.
3. Preheat griddle to medium-high heat and brush with olive oil.
4. Place kebabs on griddle. Cook, turning each kebab one-quarter turn every 1½ to 2 minutes, until meat is well browned all over, grill-marked, and registers 120ºF (49ºC) to 125ºF (52ºC) (for medium-rare), about 7 minutes, or 130ºF (54ºC) to 135ºF (57ºC) (for medium), about 8 minutes. Transfer kebabs to serving platter; squeeze lemon wedges over kebabs, if using; and serve.

New York Strip with Sauce

Prep time: 8 minutes | Cook time: 15 minutes | Serves 4 to 6

For the Poblano Worcestershire Sauce:

3 poblano chiles	1 tablespoon freshly squeezed lime juice
2 white or red un-peeled onions, halved	1 tablespoon roasted garlic
Oil and salt, for coating	1 tablespoon honey
3 tablespoons vinegar	2 pounds (907 g) New York strip steak
2 tablespoons soy sauce	

1. Preheat griddle to medium-high heat.
2. To make the sauce: Toss the poblanos and onions in oil and salt. Cook over high heat, turning occasionally, until they are completely blackened, about 10 minutes for the poblanos and a little longer for the onions. Transfer with tongs to a bowl, then tightly cover with plastic wrap to allow them to steam in their own heat and to cool enough to handle. Peel the skin from the chiles with your fingers, but don't worry if some burnt bits remain. Remove and discard the stems and seeds. Cut the peel and root end from the onions.
3. Place the chiles and onions in a blender together with the vinegar, soy sauce, lime juice, garlic, and honey and blend until completely smooth. The sauce can be stored in a covered container in the refrigerator for up to 2 weeks.
4. Coat the steaks generously with the sauce and let them marinate for 1 hour. Place the steaks over high heat and cook about 5 minutes per side, until an instant-read meat thermometer, placed in the thickest part of one steak, reads 125°F (52°C). Use tongs to sear the edges of the meat as well. Transfer to a cutting board and let rest for 10 minutes. Slice against the grain and serve, passing additional sauce at the table.

Lamb Chops with Apricot

Prep time: 6 minutes | Cook time: 19 minutes | Serves 4

Apricot–Chamomile Chutney	¼ cup honey, plus more for garnish
Oil, for coating	1 cup water
1 white or red onion, chopped	2 tablespoons chopped mint leaves
1 cup dried apricots, chopped	2 tablespoons chopped toasted un-salted almonds
1 tablespoon dried chamomile, plus more for garnish	Juice of 1 lemon (about 3 tablespoons)
2 whole star anise	2½ pounds (1.1 kg) lamb loin chops, at least 1 inch thick
3 green or white cardamom pods, with seeds removed	Salt, for seasoning

1. Preheat griddle to medium-high heat and brush with oil.
2. To make the chutney: Add the onion and cook until tender, about 5 minutes. Add the apricots, chamomile, star anise, cardamom, honey, and water. Cook until almost all of the liquid has cooked off and the mixture is thick and syrupy. (The mixture can be made to this stage up to 5 days in advance and refrigerated in a covered container.) Discard the star anise. Stir in the mint, almonds, and lemon juice.
3. Score the fatty edge of each lamb chop by cutting shallow crosshatched slices into it.
4. Salt the chops well, then place them over high heat and sear on all sides (use tongs to crisp up the fat on the edges), about 2 minutes per side. Move to medium heat and cook, turning often, until just past medium-rare (about 135°F (57°C) on an instant-read meat thermometer), about 5 minutes more in total. Transfer to a serving platter and drizzle with honey, sprinkle with chamomile, and serve with warm chutney alongside.

Lamb Burgers with Squash Salad

Prep time: 30 minutes | Cook time: 20 minutes | Serves 4

For the Summer Squash Salad:

Oil, for frying, plus 6 tablespoons
2 pounds (907 g) summer squash, thinly sliced
8 radishes, sliced paper-thin
4 jalapeño chiles, stemmed, seeded, and minced
Juice of 1 lemon (about 3 tablespoons)
6 tablespoons oil
1 teaspoon pepper
½ teaspoon salt
2 tablespoons minced cilantro leaves

For the Feta–Yogurt Sauce:

½ cup crumbled feta cheese
½ cup plain whole-milk yogurt
1 garlic clove, minced
Juice and zest of ½ lemon
1 tablespoon minced fennel fronds (may substitute minced tarragon leaves)
1 tablespoon minced parsley leaves
1 teaspoon pepper
Lamb Burgers
Oil, for coating
½ red onion, minced
2 garlic cloves, minced
1 pound (454 g) ground lamb
2 tablespoons chopped fennel fronds (may substitute chopped tarragon leaves)
2 tablespoons chopped parsley leaves
1 teaspoon ground cumin
1 teaspoon celery seed
¼ teaspoon ground cinnamon
Salt, for seasoning
4 hamburger buns, toasted

1. Preheat griddle to medium-high heat and brush with oil.
2. To make the salad: Add half of the zucchini and fry until golden brown. Remove with a slotted spoon and place on a plate lined with paper towels. When it has cooled, add the fried zucchini to a bowl with the remaining raw zucchini, radishes, and jalapeños. In a small bowl, whisk the lemon juice and 6 tablespoons oil with the pepper and salt and add to the salad, tossing to coat. Sprinkle the cilantro on top.

3. To make the sauce: In a small bowl, mix the feta and yogurt with a fork until smooth. Add the garlic, lemon juice and zest, fennel, parsley, and pepper. The sauce can be stored in a covered container in the refrigerator for up to 3 days.
4. To make the burgers: Place over high heat and add the onion and garlic. Cook until they soften and start to brown, then transfer to a bowl. When the onion and garlic are no longer hot to the touch, add the lamb, fennel, parsley, cumin, celery seed, and cinnamon and mix well with your hands. Divide the mixture into four patties.
5. Salt the burgers just before grilling. Cook over high heat for 1½ to 2 minutes per side to get good grill marks. Move to medium heat and cook to the desired doneness, 2 to 4 minutes more per side (the cooking time will vary with burger thickness).
6. To serve, place the burgers on the buns and top with the sauce and the salad, passing extra sauce and salad at the table.

Lamb Loin Rib Chops

Prep time: 10 minutes | Cook time: 15 minutes | Serves 4

8 (4-ounce / 113-g) lamb rib or loin chops, 1¼ to 1½ inches thick, trimmed
2 tablespoons extra-virgin olive oil
Salt and pepper, to taste

1. Preheat griddle to medium-high heat and brush with olive oil.
2. Rub chops with oil and season with salt and pepper. Place chops on griddle and cook until well browned, about 2 minutes per side. Slide chops to griddle and continue to cook until meat registers 120ºF (49ºC) to 125ºF (52ºC) (for medium-rare) or 130ºF (54ºC) to 135ºF (57ºC) (for medium), 2 to 4 minutes per side. Transfer chops to large platter, tent with aluminum foil, and let rest for 5 minutes before serving.

Chicken Breasts with Garlic

Prep time: 7 minutes | Cook time: 45 minutes | Serves 4

6 tablespoons olive oil
2 tablespoons lemon juice
1 tablespoon minced fresh parsley
1¼ teaspoons sugar
1 teaspoon Dijon mustard
Salt and pepper, to taste
2 tablespoons water
3 garlic cloves, minced
4 (6- to 8-ounce / 170- to 227-g) boneless, skinless chicken breasts, trimmed

1. Whisk water, garlic, remaining 3 tablespoons oil, remaining 1 tablespoon lemon juice, remaining 1 teaspoon sugar, 1½ teaspoons salt, and ½ teaspoon pepper together in bowl. Place marinade and chicken in 1-gallon zipper-lock bag and toss to coat; press out as much air as possible and seal bag. Refrigerate for at least 30 minutes or up to 1 hour, flipping bag every 15 minutes.
2. Preheat griddle to medium-high heat and brush with olive oil.
3. Remove chicken from bag, allowing excess marinade to drip off. Place chicken on griddle, smooth side down. Cook until bottom of chicken just begins to develop light grill marks and is no longer translucent, 6 to 9 minutes.
4. Flip chicken and rotate. Cover and continue to cook until chicken is opaque and firm to touch and registers 140ºF (60ºC), 6 to 9 minutes longer.
5. Move chicken to griddle and cook until dark grill marks appear on both sides and chicken registers 160ºF (71ºC), 2 to 6 minutes longer.
6. Transfer chicken to carving board, tent with aluminum foil, and let rest for 5 to 10 minutes. Slice each breast on bias into ¼-inch-thick slices and transfer to individual plates. Drizzle with reserved sauce and serve.

Rack of Lamb with Thyme

Prep time: 10 minutes | Cook time: 35 minutes | Serves 4 to 6

4 teaspoons vegetable oil
4 teaspoons minced fresh rosemary
2 teaspoons minced fresh thyme
2 garlic cloves, minced
2 (1½- to 1¾-pound / 680- to 794-g) racks of lamb (8 ribs each), trimmed and frenched
Salt and pepper, to taste

1. Combine 1 tablespoon oil, rosemary, thyme, and garlic in bowl; set aside. Pat lamb dry with paper towels, rub with remaining 1 teaspoon oil, and season with salt and pepper.
2. Preheat griddle to medium-high heat and brush with olive oil.
3. Place lamb, bone side up, on griddle with meaty side of racks very close to, but not quite over, hot coals or lit burner. Cook until meat is lightly browned, faint grill marks appear, and fat has begun to render, 8 to 10 minutes.
4. Flip racks bone side down and slide to hotter part of grill. Cook until well browned, 3 to 4 minutes. Brush racks with herb mixture, flip bone side up, and cook until well browned, 3 to 4 minutes. Stand racks up, leaning them against each other for support, and cook until bottom is well browned and meat registers 120ºF (49ºC) to 125ºF (52ºC) (for medium-rare) or 130ºF (54ºC) to 135ºF (57ºC) (for medium), 3 to 8 minutes.
5. Transfer lamb to carving board, tent with aluminum foil, and let rest for 15 to 20 minutes. Cut between ribs to separate chops and serve.

Lamb Kofte with Sauce

Prep time: 30 minutes | Cook time: 30 minutes | Serves 4 to 6

For the Yogurt-Garlic Sauce:

1 cup plain whole-milk yogurt	2 tablespoons tahini
2 tablespoons lemon juice	1 garlic clove, minced
	½ teaspoon salt

For the Kofte:

½ cup pine nuts	cinnamon
4 garlic cloves, peeled	1½ pounds (680 g) ground lamb
1½ teaspoons hot smoked paprika	½ cup grated onion, drained
1 teaspoon salt	
1 teaspoon ground cumin	1/3 cup minced fresh parsley
½ teaspoon pepper	1/3 cup minced fresh mint
¼ teaspoon ground coriander	1½ teaspoons unflavored gelatin
¼ teaspoon ground cloves	1 (13 by 9-inch) disposable aluminum roasting pan (if using charcoal)
1/8 teaspoon ground nutmeg	
1/8 teaspoon ground	

1. Whisk all ingredients together in bowl.
2. Process pine nuts, garlic, paprika, salt, cumin, pepper, coriander, cloves, nutmeg, and cinnamon into coarse paste in food processor, 30 to 45 seconds; transfer to large bowl. Add lamb, onion, parsley, mint, and gelatin to bowl and knead with your hands until thoroughly combined and mixture feels slightly sticky, about 2 minutes.
3. Divide mixture into 8 equal portions. Shape each portion into 5-inch-long cylinder about 1 inch in diameter. Using eight 12-inch metal skewers, thread 1 cylinder onto each skewer, pressing gently to adhere. Transfer skewers to lightly greased baking sheet, cover with plastic wrap, and refrigerate for 1 hour or up to 24 hours.
4. Preheat griddle to medium-high heat and brush with olive oil.
5. Place skewers on griddle (directly over coals if using charcoal) at 45-degree angle to grate bars. Cook until browned and meat easily releases from griddle, 4 to 7 minutes. Flip skewers and continue to cook until browned on second side and meat registers 160ºF (71ºC), about 6 minutes. Transfer skewers to platter and serve, passing yogurt-garlic sauce separately.

Beef Chuck Steaks with Chile

Prep time: 9 minutes | Cook time: 30 minutes | Serves 4

1 tablespoon kosher salt	coriander
1 tablespoon chipotle chile powder	½ teaspoon granulated garlic
1 teaspoon unsweetened cocoa powder	1 (2½- to 3-pound / 1.1- to 1.4-kg) boneless beef chuck-eye roast
1 teaspoon packed brown sugar	2 tablespoons vegetable oil
½ teaspoon ground	

1. Combine salt, chile powder, cocoa, sugar, coriander, and garlic in bowl. Separate roast into 2 pieces along natural seam. Turn each piece on its side and cut in half lengthwise against grain. Remove silverskin and trim fat to ¼-inch thickness. Pat steaks dry with paper towels and rub with spice mixture. Transfer steaks to 1-gallon zipper-lock bag and refrigerate for at least 6 hours or up to 24 hours.
2. Preheat griddle to medium-high heat and brush with olive oil.
3. Brush steaks all over with oil. Place steaks on griddle and cook until well charred on both sides, about 5 minutes per side. Move steaks to griddle and continue to cook until steaks register 120ºF (49ºC) to 125ºF (52ºC) (for medium-rare) or 130ºF (54ºC) to 135ºF (57ºC) (for medium), 5 to 8 minutes.
4. Transfer steaks to carving board, tent loosely with aluminum foil, and let rest for 10 minutes. Slice steaks thin against grain and serve.

Grouper

Prep time: 8 minutes | Cook time: 10 minutes | Serves 2

1 (2- to 3-pound / 0.9- to 1.4-kg) whole grouper, scaled and gutted
Oil and salt, for coating

1. Ask your fishmonger to remove the backbone, or you can do it yourself. To remove it yourself, place the fish skin side up on a cutting board, with the cavity spread open. Run a sharp knife along both sides of the spine from head to tail, releasing the flesh from the spine without cutting through the skin. Use kitchen shears to remove the backbone.
2. Preheat griddle to medium-high heat and brush with olive oil.
3. Rub the fish on both sides with oil and salt. Place the fish skin side down over high heat. Top with a cast-iron pan or plancha to weight it down. Allow to cook for 2 to 3 minutes, or until the fish easily lifts from the griddle. Watch the tail and the head, since they can snap off and you don't want to lose them. Using tongs and a thin metal fish spatula—or two metal spatulas—flip the fish onto an oiled sizzling plancha and cook, flesh side down, for another 2 to 3 minutes. Check to make sure the fish is cooked through, then transfer to a platter and serve.

Basil Lobster Tails with Butter

Prep time: 5 minutes | Cook time: 6 minutes | Serves 4

4 lobster tails (cut in half lengthwise)
3 tablespoons olive oil
For the Lime Basil Butter:
1 stick unsalted butter, softened
½ bunch basil, roughly chopped
1 lime, zested and
Lime wedges (to serve)
Sea salt, to taste

juiced
2 cloves garlic, minced
¼ teaspoon red pepper flakes

1. Add the butter ingredients to a mixing bowl and combine; set aside until ready to use.
2. Preheat griddle to medium-high heat.
3. Drizzle the lobster tail halves with olive oil and season with salt and pepper.
4. Place the lobster tails, flesh-side down, on the griddle.
5. Allow to cook until opaque, about 3 minutes, flip and cook another 3 minutes.
6. Add a dollop of the lime basil butter during the last minute of cooking.
7. Serve immediately.

Chili Crab Legs

Prep time: 5 minutes | Cook time: 5 minutes | Serves 4

4 pounds (1.8 kg) king crab legs, cooked
2 tablespoons chili oil

1. Preheat griddle to high.
2. Brush both sides of crab legs with chili oil and place on griddle. Tent with foil.
3. Cook 4 to 5 minutes, turning once.
4. Transfer to plates and serve with drawn butter.

Crab Cakes with Mayo

Prep time: 10 minutes | Cook time: 15 minutes | Serves 4

1 pound (454 g) lump crab meat
½ cup panko bread crumbs
⅓ cup mayonnaise
1 egg, beaten
2 tablespoons dijon mustard
2 teaspoons Worcestershire sauce
½ teaspoon paprika
½ teaspoon salt
¼ teaspoon black pepper
3 tablespoons vegetable oil

1. Preheat griddle to medium heat.
2. In a large bowl, combine the crab, bread crumbs, mayo, egg, mustard Worcestershire sauce, paprika, salt and pepper. Mix well to combine.
3. Form the crab mixture into 4 large balls and flatten them slightly.
4. Add the oil to the griddle and cook the crab cakes for approximately 5 minutes per side or until browned and crispy. Serve immediately.

Shrimp with Parsley

Prep time: 15 minutes | Cook time: 8 minutes | Serves 6

1½ pounds (680 g) uncooked jumbo	shrimp, peeled and deveined

For the Marinade:

2 tablespoons fresh parsley	powder
1 bay leaf, dried	¼ teaspoon cayenne pepper
1 teaspoon chili powder	¼ cup olive oil
1 teaspoon garlic	¼ teaspoon salt
	⅛ teaspoon pepper

1. Add marinade ingredients to a food processor and process until smooth.
2. Transfer marinade to a large mixing bowl.
3. Fold in shrimp and toss to coat; refrigerate, covered, 30 minutes.
4. Thread shrimp onto metal skewers.
5. Preheat griddle to medium heat.
6. Cook 5 to 6 minutes, flipping once, until shrimp turn opaque pink.
7. Serve immediately.

Shrimp Skewers with Pineapple

Prep time: 20 minutes | Cook time: 5 minutes | Serves 4

1½ pounds (680 g) uncooked jumbo shrimp, peeled and deveined	¼ cup freshly squeezed orange juice
½ cup light coconut milk	¼ cup freshly squeezed lime juice (from about 2 large limes)
1 tablespoon cilantro, chopped	¾ pound (340 g) pineapple, cut into 1 inch chunks
4 teaspoons Tabasco Original Red Sauce	Olive oil, for grilling
2 teaspoons soy sauce	

1. Combine the coconut milk, cilantro, Tabasco sauce, soy sauce, orange juice, lime juice. Add the shrimp and toss to coat.
2. Cover and place in the refrigerator to marinate for 1 hour.
3. Thread shrimp and pineapple onto metal skewers, alternating each.

4. Preheat griddle to medium heat.
5. Cook 5 to 6 minutes, flipping once, until shrimp turn opaque pink.
6. Serve immediately.

Shrimp with Sauce

Prep time: 6 minutes | Cook time: 10 minutes | Serves 4 to 6

For the Fermented Pineapple–Peanut Sauce

1 cup roasted unsalted peanuts	1 tablespoon salt, plus more for seasoning
10 dried chiles de árbol, stemmed and seeded	1 ripe pineapple, cored, and cut into small chunks
1 cup oil, plus more for coating	2 pounds (907 g) unpeeled jumbo shrimp
2 tablespoons honey, plus more for seasoning	Oil and salt, for coating

1. To make the sauce: Put the peanuts, chiles, oil, honey, and salt in a blender and blend until smooth. Add the pineapple, cover with plastic wrap, and place in the sun or in a warm area of your kitchen for at least 3 hours, or until the liquid begins to bubble. Blend the mixture until smooth, then transfer to a medium-mesh strainer or cheesecloth and push through with a rubber spatula, discarding the solids. Season with more salt and/or honey, if needed. Store, covered, in the refrigerator for up to 2 weeks.
2. Preheat griddle to medium-high heat and brush with olive oil.
3. Using scissors, cut through the backs of the shrimp shells and remove the dark vein with a small knife (this will also make it easier to peel the shrimp). Toss the shrimp with oil and salt and place over medium heat. Grill just until opaque, 3 to 4 minutes per side (check by cutting into one, and remove the shrimp from the heat the minute they're no longer translucent in the middle). Serve the shrimp whole with the sauce drizzled on top or passed alongside.

Spiced Snapper with Salsa

Prep time: 10 minutes | Cook time: 20 minutes | Serves 4

2 red snappers, cleaned
Sea salt, to taste
1/3 cup tandoori spice
Olive oil, plus more
For the Salsa:
1 ripe but firm mango, peeled and chopped
1 small red onion, thinly sliced

for grill
Extra-virgin olive oil, for drizzling
Lime wedges, for serving

1 bunch cilantro, coarsely chopped
3 tablespoons fresh lime juice

1. Toss mango, onion, cilantro, lime juice, and a big pinch of salt in a medium mixing bowl; drizzle with a bit of olive oil and toss again to coat.
2. Place snapper on a cutting board and pat dry with paper towels. Cut slashes crosswise on a diagonal along the body every 2" on both sides, with a sharp knife, cutting all the way down to the bones.
3. Season fish generously inside and out with salt. Coat fish with tandoori spice.
4. Preheat griddle medium-high heat and brush with oil.
5. Grill fish for 10 minutes, undisturbed, until skin is puffed and charred.
6. Flip and grill fish until the other side is lightly charred and skin is puffed, about 8 to 12 minutes.
7. Transfer to a platter.
8. Top with mango salad and serve with lime wedges.

Cilantro Fish with Lime

Prep time: 5 minutes | Cook time: 6 minutes | Serves 4

4 cups oil, plus more as needed
4 garlic cloves
1 white onion, quartered
1 jalapeño chile, stemmed, halved, and seeded
1 (3- to 5-pound / 1.4- to 2.3-kg) whole

fish, such as snapper, striped bass, or hogfish, scaled and gutted
Salt, for seasoning
1 bunch cilantro (leaves only)
Juice of 2 limes (about ¼ cup)

1. Preheat griddle to medium-high heat and brush with olive oil. Add the garlic, onion, and jalapeño and cook until the garlic is cooked through but not burnt, about 3 minutes. Use tongs to remove the garlic and set aside.
2. Using a sharp knife, cut 2 or 3 deep slits into both sides of the fish, being careful not to cut through the bone.
3. Push the onion and jalapeño to the sides of the griddle and add the fish. Cook until the skin is crisp and golden brown, 5 to 6 minutes, then flip the fish with a metal spatula and cook for another 5 minutes, or just until cooked through (cut into it; the flesh should be opaque and flake with a fork). Keep stirring the onion and jalapeño as well; they should be tender and browned by the time the fish is cooked. Remove the fish with two slotted spoons and drain on a wire rack or on a plate lined with paper towels. Season with salt.
4. Scoop the garlic, onion, and jalapeño into a food processor or mortar and pestle and add the cilantro and lime juice. Puree until smooth, season with salt, and serve warm with the fish.

Lime Tilapia and Corn Tilapia

Prep time: 10 minutes | Cook time: 10 minutes | Serves 4

4 fillets tilapia
2 tablespoons honey
4 limes, thinly sliced
2 ears corn, shucked
2 tablespoons fresh

cilantro leaves
¼ cup olive oil
Kosher salt, to taste
Freshly ground black pepper, to taste

1. Preheat griddle to high.
2. Cut 4 squares of foil about 12" long.
3. Top each piece of foil with a piece of tilapia.
4. Brush tilapia with honey and top with lime, corn and cilantro.
5. Drizzle with olive oil and season with sea salt and pepper.
6. Cook until tilapia is cooked through and corn tender, about 15 minutes.

Spinach Halibut with Olives

Prep time: 10 minutes | Cook time: 10 minutes | Serves 4

4 (6-ounce / 170-g) halibut fillets
⅓ cup olive oil
4 cups baby spinach
¼ cup lemon juice
2 ounces (57 g) pitted black olives, halved

2 tablespoons flat leaf parsley, chopped
2 teaspoons fresh dill, chopped
Lemon wedges, to serve

1. Preheat griddle to medium heat.
2. Toss spinach with lemon juice in a mixing bowl and set aside.
3. Brush fish with olive oil and cook for 3-4 minutes per side, or until cooked through.
4. Remove from heat, cover with foil and let rest for 5 minutes.
5. Add remaining oil and cook spinach for 2 minutes, or until just wilted. Remove from heat.
6. Toss with olives and herbs, then transfer to serving plates with fish, and serve with lemon wedges.

Lemony Swordfish Skewers

Prep time: 20 minutes | Cook time: 10 minutes | Serves 4

1 (½-pound / 227-g) skinless swordfish fillet
2 teaspoons lemon zest
3 tablespoons lemon juice
½ cup finely chopped parsley
2 teaspoons garlic,

minced
¾ teaspoon sea salt
¼ teaspoon black pepper
2 tablespoons ex-tra-virgin olive oil, plus extra for serving
½ teaspoon red pepper flakes
3 lemons, cut into slices

1. Preheat griddle to medium-high.
2. Combine lemon zest, parsley, garlic, ¼ teaspoon of the salt, and pepper in a small bowl with a fork to make gremolata and set aside.
3. Mix swordfish pieces with reserved lem-on juice, olive oil, red pepper flakes, and remaining salt.

4. Thread swordfish and lemon slices, alter-nating each, onto the metal skewers.
5. Grill skewers 8 to 10 minutes, flipping halfway through, or until fish is cooked through.
6. Place skewers on a serving platter and sprinkle with gremolata.
7. Drizzle with olive oil and serve.

Tuna Steaks with Ginger

Prep time: 6 minutes | Cook time: 14 minutes | Serves 4

For the Rub:

2 tablespoons salt
2 teaspoons cayenne pepper
2 teaspoons sweet paprika
1 teaspoon ground white pepper
1 teaspoon celery salt
1 tablespoon peeled and finely grated fresh ginger

1 large garlic clove, grated
2 tablespoons oil
1 tablespoon honey
2 (12-ounce / 340-g) tuna steaks, about 1½ inches thick
Oil, for drizzling
Lemon wedges, for serving

1. To make the rub: Mix the salt, cayenne, paprika, white pepper, celery salt, ginger, garlic, oil, and honey in a small bowl.
2. Cover the tuna with the wet rub, mas-sage for about 3 minutes, then refriger-ate uncovered for 30 to 60 minutes.
3. Preheat griddle to medium-high heat and brush with olive oil.
4. When you are ready to cook, place the tuna steaks on the griddle, with at least 2 inches between them.
5. Using a thin metal fish spatula, flip the tuna after 2 minutes, being careful not to let the fish flake apart. Cook for an-other 2 minutes. You want to check for doneness without cutting into the fish, so watch the thick edges of the fish; pink should be the dominant color.
6. Transfer to a cutting board and let the fish rest for 4 to 5 minutes. Slice the tuna along (not against) the grain. Tuna is a lean fish, so you can brush a little warm oil over it as it sits so it doesn't dry out. Eat it hot or store, covered, in the refrig-erator for up to 8 hours. Serve cool or at room temperature. Hot or cool, drizzle it with oil and serve it with the lemon.

Lemony Rainbow Trout

Prep time: 7 minutes | Cook time: 15 minutes | Serves 4

Cumin and Burnt Citrus Vinaigrette
1½ tablespoons cumin seeds
3 oranges
3 lemons
1½ cups oil, plus more for coating
3 tablespoons honey, plus more for coating
¼ cup vinegar
½ shallot, grated
1½ teaspoons salt
½ teaspoon Mexican oregano
4 whole rainbow trout, 12 to 16 ounces (340 to 454 g) each, scaled and gutted
Oil and salt, for coating

1. Preheat griddle to medium-high heat and brush with olive oil.
2. To make the vinaigrette: Add the cumin to griddle and shake over medium heat until toasted and fragrant, about 2 minutes. Grind until very fine in a spice grinder or blender and set aside.
3. Zest 1 orange and 1 lemon and set zest aside. Cut all the oranges and lemons in half and toss in about 1 tablespoon each of oil and honey, just enough to coat. Place the citrus cut side down on the griddle over medium heat and grill until nicely charred and fragrant, 1 to 2 minutes. Once they have cooled, juice to get about 1½ cups juice.
4. Combine the juice, vinegar, shallot, orange and lemon zest, cumin, salt, oregano, and remaining 2 tablespoons honey in a bowl. Whisk, until the salt and honey have dissolved. While whisking, slowly pour in the 1½ cups oil and continue to whisk until emulsified. The vinaigrette can be stored in a covered container in the refrigerator for up to 1 week.
5. To cook the trout: Open and gently press each fish so it lies flat. Rub the fish with oil and salt. Place skin side down over medium heat and cook until the skin is browned and crisp and the flesh turns opaque, 4 to 5 minutes. Serve the fish folded back over (so it looks again like a whole fish).

Beer Whitefish with Mayo

Prep time: 5 minutes | Cook time: 10 minutes | Serves 4

For the Roasted Garlic Mayo:
3 egg yolks, at room temperature
1 tablespoon freshly squeezed lemon or lime juice
1¾ cups oil
2 tablespoons roasted garlic
2 teaspoons salt

For the Beer-Battered Fish:
5 cups oil, plus more as needed
1½ cups all-purpose flour, plus more for coating
1 teaspoon ancho chile powder
1 teaspoon salt, plus more for seasoning
½ teaspoon baking soda
1 (12-ounce / 340-g) can dark beer
2 pounds (907 g) boneless, skinless whitefish fillets, such as cod or amberjack, cut into 1½-inch-thick strips

1. To make the mayo: Combine the egg yolks and lemon juice in a blender or food processor. Blend for 30 seconds and while continuing to blend, slowly drizzle in the oil; the mixture should become thick and emulsified. Add the garlic and salt and blend just to combine. The mayo can be stored, covered, in the refrigerator for up to 3 days.
2. To prepare the fish: Preheat griddle to medium-high heat and brush with olive oil.
3. Combine the flour, chile powder, salt, and baking soda in a large bowl. While whisking, add the beer slowly and continue whisking until smooth; it should have the consistency of pancake batter. Season the fish fillets with salt, coat with plain flour, and dip into the beer batter. Let any excess batter drip back into the bowl and gently lay the fish in the oil (work in batches and don't let the fish pieces touch). Cook for 2 to 3 minutes per side (use a metal spatula or slotted spoon to flip), until deep golden brown and crisp. Remove with a slotted spoon and drain on a wire rack or on a plate lined with paper towels. Serve with the garlic mayo.

Potato Snapper Ceviche with Lime

Prep time: 15 minutes | Cook time: 15 minutes | Serves 4

1 small fennel bulb, with fronds attached
1 teaspoon salt, plus more for seasoning
1 tablespoon sugar
Vinegar, for pickling
¼ cup oil
¼ cup honey
1 large sweet potato, sliced lengthwise into ¾-inch slices
5 limes
2 oranges
2 mandarins
1 grapefruit

1½ pounds (680 g) boneless, skinless snapper or any other whitefish
½ small red onion, sliced paper thin
2 plum tomatoes, diced
½ Granny Smith apple, peeled, cored, and cut into matchstick-size batons
¼ cup chopped cilantro leaves

1. Trim root and stalks from the fennel bulb, cut into quarters, and remove and discard the core. Slice paper thin with a mandoline or sharp knife. Cut the fronds from the stalks, mince, and set aside. Combine the fennel with the salt, sugar, and enough vinegar to cover. Set aside to pickle while prepping the remaining ingredients.
2. Mix the oil and honey together in a large bowl. Toss the sweet potato in the oil-honey mixture to coat, letting any excess liquid drip back into the bowl. Season the sweet potatoes with salt and grill over medium heat until they are brown and caramelized and are easily pierced with a fork, about 5 minutes per side. Use tongs to transfer to a bowl, then tightly cover with plastic wrap to allow them to steam in their own heat as they cool. Once they are cool enough to handle, cut into cubes.
3. Preheat griddle to medium-high heat and brush with olive oil.
4. Set aside 2 limes and cut all the remaining citrus in half. Brush the cut sides with the remaining oil–honey mixture and place them cut side down over medium heat until they are nicely charred, about 2 minutes. Once they have cooled, juice all of them plus the 2 fresh limes that were set aside, and strain.

5. Cut the fish into ½-inch cubes and salt lightly. Add the citrus juice and mix well. Add the sweet potato, drained pickled fennel, onion, tomato, apple, cilantro, and 2 tablespoons of the fennel fronds. Serve immediately.

Shrimp with Lime

Prep time: 9 minutes | Cook time: 43 minutes | Serves 4

For the Rub:

1 tablespoon coriander seeds
1 tablespoon whole allspice berries
½ tablespoon cumin seeds
1 teaspoon black peppercorns
1 teaspoon ground cloves
1 teaspoon sweet pa-

prika
1 teaspoon cayenne pepper
Zest of 2 limes
1 tablespoon salt
16 jumbo shrimp, peeled and deveined
Honey, as needed
4 limes, halved, for serving

1. To make the rub: Combine the coriander, allspice, cumin, and peppercorns in a heavy pan and toast over medium heat until fragrant, about 3 minutes. Grind to a fine powder in a spice grinder or blender and mix in the cloves, paprika, cayenne, lime zest, and salt.
2. Preheat griddle to medium-high heat and brush with olive oil.
3. Coat the shrimp liberally with the spice mixture. The shrimp's own moisture should help the rub adhere, but if not, add a little honey. Place 4 shrimp on each of 4 metal skewers (if using wood skewers, soak for an hour before using) and smoke for 30 to 40 minutes. Just before serving, place the shrimp over high heat for a minute per side to heat through. (You can also grill the shrimp without smoking; grill over medium heat for about 3 minutes per side, just until cooked through.) Grill the limes and serve with the shrimp.

Clam and Shrimp Bouillabaisse

Prep time: 5 minutes | Cook time: 10 minutes | Serves 4

For the Bouillabaisse:

1 large tomato
½ small fennel bulb, with fronds attached
¼ cup oil
½ white onion, minced
4 garlic cloves, sliced
2-inch piece fresh ginger, peeled and sliced
2 tablespoons tarragon leaves, chopped
6 basil leaves, chopped
4 cups fish stock (I like Aneto brand)
Salt and pepper, for seasoning
½ pound (227 g) small hardshell clams, such as littleneck or Manila, scrubbed and

rinsed of all sand
½ pound (227 g) unpeeled head-on large shrimp
1½ pounds (680 g) boneless, skinless whitefish fillets, such as cod, sea bass, or snapper
Tarragon–Garlic Toasts
6 tablespoons oil, plus more for brushing
3 tablespoons minced garlic
Generous pinch of salt
¼ cup minced tarragon leaves
Eight ½-inch-thick slices French bread

1. Preheat griddle to medium-high heat and brush with olive oil.
2. To make the bouillabaisse: Place the tomato directly onto the griddle until it blackens. Remove to a plate and set aside.
3. Trim root and stalks from the fennel bulb, cut into quarters, remove and discard the core, and mince. Cut the fronds from the stalks, mince, and set aside.
4. Add the onion, garlic, ginger, and minced fennel and cook until the vegetables are soft and golden brown, about 5 minutes. Rub most of the burnt bits off the tomato and add to the griddle, crushing with the back of a spoon. Add 2 tablespoons of the fennel fronds, the tarragon, basil, fish stock, and salt and pepper. Cover and bring to a boil.
5. Add the clams to griddle, cover, and cook until the shells open (discard any that don't open). Place the shrimp and fish directly on the griddle, over high heat, and cook just until charred on both sides.
6. To make the toasts: Heat the oil in griddle over medium heat. Add the garlic and salt and cook until the garlic starts to turn golden brown. While the garlic cooks, toast the bread over medium heat until the slices are golden brown. Add the tarragon to the oil, stir well, and brush the slices generously with oil. Serve immediately with the bouillabaisse.

Salmon Fillets with Broccolini

Prep time: 10 minutes | Cook time: 12 minutes | Serves 2

2 (6-ounce / 170-g) salmon fillets, skin removed
2 tablespoons butter, unsalted
2 basil leaves, minced

1 garlic clove, minced
6 ounces (170 g) broccolini
2 teaspoons olive oil
Sea salt, to taste

1. Blend butter, basil, and garlic together until well-incorporated. Form into a ball and place in refrigerator until ready to serve.
2. Preheat griddle to medium-high heat.
3. Season both sides of the salmon fillets with salt and set aside.
4. Add broccolini, a pinch of salt, and olive oil to a bowl, toss to coat, and set aside.
5. Brush griddle with olive oil, and cook salmon, skin side down, for 12 minutes. Turn the salmon and cook for an additional 4 minutes. Remove from the griddle and allow to rest while the broccolini cooks.
6. Add the broccolini to the griddle, turning occasionally, until slightly charred, about 6 minutes.
7. Top each salmon fillet with a slice of basil butter and serve with a side of broccolini.

Lobster and Corn Butter Salad

Prep time: 4 minutes | Cook time: 10 minutes | Serves 4

4 ears of corn, shucked
4 spring onions, white and green parts (may substitute large scallions)
Oil, for coating
Salt, for coating and seasoning
4 large lobster tails (about 8 ounces / 227 g each), with meat extracted from the shells
1 serrano chile, stemmed and thinly sliced into rounds
3 celery stalks, thinly sliced on the bias
½ cup basil leaves, coarsely chopped
¼ cup dill, coarsely chopped
¼ cup mint leaves, coarsely chopped
½ cup celery leaves, coarsely chopped
Citrus–Brown Butter Vinaigrette
2 oranges
2 limes
Oil and honey, for coating
½ cup (1 stick) butter

1. Preheat griddle to medium-high heat and brush with olive oil.
2. Toss the corn and spring onions with oil and salt and grill over medium heat until nicely charred, about 4 minutes. Toss the lobster meat with oil and salt and cook over medium heat, about 2 minutes per side or just until cooked through. As they finish cooking, transfer the vegetables and lobster to a plate and let cool to room temperature. Cut the kernels from the cobs, coarsely chop the onions, and cut the lobster into pieces about 1 inch square. Add to a large bowl, together with the chile, sliced celery, basil, dill, mint, and chopped celery leaves. Season with salt.
3. To make the vinaigrette: Cut the oranges and limes in half, toss with the oil and honey, and place cut side down over medium heat. Grill until charred, about 3 minutes, and transfer to a plate. Meanwhile, heat the butter in a small saucepan over medium heat until it begins to smell nutty and turn a very light brown (if it seems to be cooking too quickly, just briefly remove from the heat). Remove the pan from the heat and squeeze the citrus into it. Whisk to emulsify and season with additional honey and/or salt. Dress the lobster salad liberally with the vinaigrette and serve.

Amberjack with Chiles

Prep time: 15 minutes | Cook time: 2 hours | Serves 4

1½ pounds (680 g) boneless, skinless amberjack fillets
1½ cups oil, plus more for coating
1 teaspoon salt, plus more for coating
4 guajillo chiles, toasted, stemmed, and seeded

1. Preheat griddle to medium-high heat and brush with olive oil.
2. Coat the amberjack with oil and salt. Cook for 2 hours. The fish should have a deeply golden color when done. Transfer the fish to a board and set aside until cool enough to handle. Using your hands, break the fish into smaller pieces and place in a covered container.
3. Add the chiles to a blender together with the 1½ cups oil and 1 teaspoon salt and blend until smooth. Strain and pour over the fish to cover. Serve right away or store, covered, in the refrigerator.

Chapter 7 Side Dishes

Fried Rice with Carrot

Prep time: 15 minutes | Cook time: 5 minutes | Serves 4

½ cup soy sauce
½ cup water
½ cup oyster sauce
2 tablespoons sesame oil
1 tablespoon sriracha (optional)
½ cup finely diced carrots
½ cup diced sweet onions
4 cloves garlic, minced
½ cup frozen peas
4 cups cooked rice, cooled
½ cup finely sliced scallions, divided
Cooking oil, as needed

1. In a medium bowl, whisk together soy sauce, water, oyster sauce, sesame oil, and sriracha, if using, and set aside.
2. Bring the griddle grill to medium-high heat and add some cooking oil to the surface. When the oil begins to shimmer, add the carrots, onions, and garlic. Cook, stirring frequently, for about 5 minutes, until the onions begin to turn translucent. Add the peas to the mixture and move to one side of the griddle grill.
3. Add cooking oil to the open space on the griddle and spread the rice out evenly in a single layer. Heat and cook the rice for 3 to 4 minutes, or until it begins to brown a bit.
4. Bring the rice together into a large, tall pile and add about half of the fried rice sauce, half of the scallions, and the cooked vegetables. Using a large spatula, mix the rice and veggies well, then spread the rice back to a single layer on the griddle, allowing the liquids to evaporate and be absorbed in the rice. As the rice absorbs the liquid from the sauce, it will darken. Continue to add fried rice sauce, flipping and mixing the rice until the liquid coats the rice.
5. Transfer the rice onto a serving platter and garnish with the remaining scallions.

Breaded Cheese Ravioli

Prep time: 5 minutes | Cook time: 8 minutes | Serves 4

12 frozen cheese ravioli
½ cup all-purpose flour
1 egg beaten with 2 tablespoons water
1 cup Italian-flavored bread crumbs
¼ cup freshly grated Parmesan cheese
1 tablespoon minced fresh parsley
Cooking oil, as needed
Marinara sauce, for dipping

1. Spread the frozen ravioli out on a plate and allow them to sit at room temperature for 15 minutes while you bring the griddle grill to medium heat.
2. Place the flour, egg mixture, and bread crumbs in three separate dishes. Dredge the ravioli in flour, then into the egg wash, and then the Italian bread crumbs to develop an even crust. Combine the Parmesan cheese and parsley in a small bowl and set aside.
3. Coat the griddle grill with cooking oil, and when the oil begins to shimmer, place the ravioli in the oil. Allow them to cook without disturbing for about 90 seconds, which will firm up the crust on one side.
4. Flip the ravioli, taking care not to knock off the breading. When the breading has set, you may need to add more oil to the griddle to promote even browning. Cook for 3 to 4 minutes per side, or until the crust gets firm and is golden brown.
5. Remove the ravioli from the griddle and sprinkle with the parsley-cheese mixture while they are still hot enough to melt the cheese. Serve with marinara sauce for dipping.

Radish Browns with Black Beans

Prep time: 10 minutes | Cook time: 13 minutes | Serves 3 to 4

1 bunch radishes, cleaned and grated
½ cup diced red bell pepper
2 cloves garlic, minced
½ cup cooked black beans, drained
1 teaspoon garlic powder
1 teaspoon onion powder
Sour cream, to serve
Coconut oil or other cooking oil, as needed
Salt and pepper, to taste

1. While your griddle grill preheats to medium, cut the tops and bottoms off the radishes. Rinse and clean them well in cold water. The quickest and easiest way to grate the radishes is with a food processor, but if you do not have one available you can use a handheld grater and get the same result.
2. Coat the griddle with a good amount of oil. When the oil begins to shimmer, add the diced red pepper and minced garlic, and cook for about 2 minutes to soften.
3. Add the shredded radishes, black beans, garlic powder, and onion powder to the vegetables, season with salt and pepper, and form a cake about ½ inch thick. Cover and allow the radishes to cook for 4 to 5 minutes, until they begin to brown.
4. Add a bit more cooking oil to the griddle and flip the cake into the new oil once it is hot. Cook for another 3 to 4 minutes, until browned. Serve with a dollop of sour cream, if desired.

Yogurt Flatbread

Prep time: 5 minutes | Cook time: 10 minutes | Serves 8

1 cup warm water
1 teaspoon sugar
1 tablespoon instant dry yeast
3 cups all-purpose flour
½ cup plain yogurt
1 tablespoon olive oil
1 teaspoon salt
Cooking oil, as needed

1. In a large bowl, stir together the warm water, sugar, and yeast. Allow the yeast to activate for about 10 minutes.
2. Add all the remaining ingredients, except the cooking oil. Stir until smooth and well combined.
3. Allow the dough to rest, covered, and rise for 1 hour. Turn the dough out onto a floured surface.
4. Bring the griddle grill to medium heat. Divide the dough into eight balls. Roll out each ball into a round about ¼ to ⅛ inch thick.
5. Add a thin coat of oil to the griddle grill and cook the dough rounds for 1 to 2 minutes per side.

Bacon and Jalapeno Cheese Corn

Prep time: 5 minutes | Cook time: 20 minutes | Serves 2

2 ears corn, shucked
½ cup cream cheese, softened
1 tablespoon smoked paprika
½ cup finely diced seeded jalapeno
6 strips thin-cut bacon

1. Smear the corn with cream cheese. This allows the jalapenos to adhere better. Dust each of the ears of corn with paprika directly onto the cream cheese.
2. Sprinkle the diced jalapenos on a cutting board or flat surface, and then roll the corn through the jalapenos, picking up as many bits of pepper as you can.
3. Start with a strip of bacon at the stalk end and wrap it around the corn. If you give the bacon a bit of a stretch, it often makes a smoother layer and adheres more tightly. Overlap the strips of bacon and wrap until the entire ear of corn is covered. Take care to wrap the bacon tightly so the cream cheese is less likely to leak out.
4. Preheat the griddle to a target temperature of about 300°F.
5. Place bacon-wrapped corn directly on the griddle and cover. Rotate the corn a quarter turn every 2 to 3 minutes. The goal is to both render the bacon and allow the corn to completely cook through.
6. The corn should be done in 15 to 18 minutes, but the slower you render the bacon, the more flavorful the corn becomes.

Cabbage Buttermilk Pancake

Prep time: 10 minutes | Cook time: 8 minutes | Serves 2 to 4

2 cups shredded cabbage	bacon or pork belly
¼ cup plus 1 tablespoon minced green onion, divided	½ cup barbecue sauce
	¼ cup hoisin sauce
	½ cup mayonnaise
2 cups Buttermilk Pancake batter	1 teaspoon mirin
4 strips thinly sliced	Black sesame seeds, for garnish

1. In a large bowl, add the shredded cabbage and green onions to the pancake batter and stir to combine.
2. Bring the griddle grill to medium heat. Cut the bacon or pork belly in half slices so you have 8 shorter pieces. Slowly cook the bacon in 2 batches of 4 strips each, in separate areas of the griddle. Adjust the heat if necessary to make sure it is cooking, but not browning and getting crispy just yet, 3 to 5 minutes. A nice pool of rendered bacon fat should be visible.
3. Flip each pile of bacon into the rendered fat and arrange the strips very close together, touching but not overlapping. Using a 1 cup measure, pour the pancake and cabbage mixture onto one of the groups of bacon. The remaining batter goes on the other.
4. Slowly cook the pancake undisturbed for about 5 minutes or until bubbles form and burst, leaving small craters where the bubbles were.
5. Run a long, sturdy spatula under the pancake, taking care to release the bacon from the griddle. When the pancake feels released and slides easily, give it a flip and do the same with the other one. Cook for 3 minutes more.
6. In a small bowl, mix the barbecue sauce with the hoisin. In a separate bowl, mix the mayonnaise with the mirin.
7. Remove the pancakes from the griddle and while they are hot, brush on a thin layer of the hoisin barbecue sauce.
8. Put the mayonnaise mixture in a squeeze bottle and adorn the top of the cabbage cakes with thin ropes of mayonnaise. Garnish with the remaining green onion and sprinkle with black sesame seeds.

Potato with Corn

Prep time: 15 minutes | Cook time: 20 minutes | Serves 4

3 baked russet potatoes, cut to 1-inch cubes	1 teaspoon pepper
	½ cup corn (optional)
½ cup cooked or frozen broccoli florets	½ cup cooked black beans (optional)
½ cup cooked or frozen diced onion	½ cup diced ham (optional)
3 cloves garlic, minced	½ cup crumbled cooked sausage (optional)
1 tablespoon garlic salt	½ cup diced bacon (optional)
1 tablespoon smoked paprika	Cooking oil, as needed

1. Bring the griddle grill to medium-high heat. Place a good amount of cooking oil on the griddle and when it begins to shimmer, add the diced potatoes in a single layer. Potato pieces will either have three or four sides depending on how they are cut, and you want to allow each of the flat sides to cook for 3 to 5 minutes, adding more oil as needed.
2. While the potatoes are cooking, sauté the broccoli, onion, and garlic for 4 to 5 minutes until lightly browned, stirring or flipping occasionally.
3. When the potatoes are crisp on the outside and creamy in the middle, 10 to 12 minutes, add the vegetable mixture to the potatoes along with the garlic salt, smoked paprika, and pepper. Cook for another 2 to 3 minutes, incorporating any optional ingredients as desired. Serve hot.

Coleslaw Egg Rolls

Prep time: 10 minutes | Cook time: 10 minutes | Serves 8

8 egg roll wrappers
4 cups bagged cole-slaw mix (shredded cabbage and carrots)
2 tablespoons ginger paste
2 tablespoons soy sauce

2 tablespoons sesame oil
1 tablespoon garlic powder
1 teaspoon ground ginger
Cooking oil, as needed

1. Keep the egg roll wrappers sealed until just before you construct the egg rolls. Mix all the other ingredients, except the cooking oil, in a large bowl, taking care to coat the veggies with all the spices.
2. Bring the griddle grill to medium heat. Cook the vegetable mixture to wilt the cabbage, soften the carrots, and release moisture from the mixture, 6 to 8 minutes. Cooking the vegetable mixture should diminish it in size by about a third. Set aside on a few paper towels to soak up any additional moisture and allow to cool to at least room temperature.
3. Egg roll wrappers are basically raw pasta sheets. They are susceptible to drying out and acting strange if exposed to air for too long, so when you work with one, keep the others covered and away from liquids. To make an egg roll, place the wrapper on a dry work surface. Spoon about ¼ cup of the vegetable mix onto the bottom third of the wrapper, leaving a border about the width of your pointer finger from the edges. Fill a small bowl with water you can dip your fingers in and finger-paint a small amount of water around the edge of the wrapper, no wider than the width of your finger. Moistening the edges of the wrapper will allow it to adhere to itself. Fold the moistened right and left sides of the wrapper toward the veggies and pinch in place. Take the wrapper side closest to you, and roll the wrapper over the veggies snugly toward the top of the wrapper. The filling should stay inside the wrapper, and the sides should be sealed. Place the egg roll seam-side down on a dry tray and repeat with the remaining ingredients.
4. Bring the griddle grill to medium-high heat. Add cooking oil, and when it begins to shimmer, place the egg rolls on the griddle with the seam sides down. Allow the egg rolls to cook without touching them for 3 to 4 minutes. This will seal the egg rolls shut. Carefully roll the egg rolls on the cooking surface to brown the other sides of the wrappers, adding more cooking oil if necessary. Since the veggies are already cooked, you are just browning the wrapper and heating the veggies back up to temperature.

Chapter 8 Desserts

Chickpeas with Cumin

Prep time: 5 minutes | Cook time: 30 minutes | Serves 2

1 (16-ounce / 454-g) can chickpeas, drained
¼ cup olive oil
1 tablespoon ground cumin
1 tablespoon smoked paprika
1 teaspoon garlic powder
1 teaspoon onion powder
1 teaspoon kosher salt, plus more to taste

1. Combine all ingredients in a large bowl.
2. Pour the mixture onto a cool griddle grill and bring the griddle to medium heat.
3. Allow the mixture to slowly come to temperature and continue to cook, stirring frequently, for up to 30 minutes or until the garbanzo beans have lost most of their moisture and become crispy and crunchy. Finish with additional salt, if desired.

Syrupy Pineapple Rings

Prep time: 5 minutes | Cook time: 6 minutes | Serves 8

1 pineapple, cored and cut into rings, or 1 (16-ounce / 454-g) can pineapple rings
¼ cup maple syrup
Juice of 1 lime
¼ teaspoon ground cinnamon
Clarified butter, or coconut oil
1 pint maple walnut ice cream, to serve
Chocolate sauce, to serve

1. Bring the griddle grill to medium heat. In a small bowl, stir together the maple syrup, lime juice, and cinnamon, and set aside.
2. Wipe a thin coat of butter or oil on the griddle grill. Place the pineapple in the oil and cook for 3 to 4 minutes, flipping frequently. Use your nose. If you start to smell something burning, it probably is, and you will need to move the pineapple to a cooler part of the griddle.
3. When the pineapple develops some golden color, brush the maple-lime syrup on both sides of the rings. Cook for another 45 seconds per side and remove.
4. Serve with a small scoop of maple walnut ice cream and a drizzle of chocolate sauce.

Strawberry Shortcake

Prep time: 5 minutes | Cook time: 12 minutes | Serves 6 to 8

4 cups strawberries (about 32)
1/3 cup sugar
1 (16-ounce / 454-g) can flaky biscuit dough
whipped cream, for garnish
Blueberries, for garnish
Butter, as needed

1. Hull and quarter the strawberries, and place them in a large bowl. Sprinkle on the sugar and stir to combine. Allow the strawberries to macerate in the sugar and release their juices, for 30 minutes, or up to 2 hours. If you wait longer than that, the berries become mushy.
2. Bring the griddle grill to medium heat and coat the surface with butter. Pop open the can of biscuits and separate them. Sometimes they come out smooshed on one side or looking asymmetrical. If this happens, flatten the biscuit slightly so it has as much surface contact with the griddle as possible.
3. Cook the biscuits in the butter for 4 to 6 minutes per side, or until golden brown and a bit risen.
4. Split the cooked biscuits in half and scoop some of the strawberries and their juices over the cut side. Top with whipped cream and blueberries, if using, add the top half of the biscuit, and enjoy.

Creamy Panna Cotta with Plums

Prep time: 5 minutes | Cook time: 15 minutes | Serves 4

2¼ cups heavy cream
1 vanilla bean, split lengthwise
1 tablespoon black peppercorns, crushed
1 cup sugar

4 sheets gelatin
4 ripe plums, pitted and halved
Honey, oil, and salt, for coating
½ cup water

1. Pour the cream into a saucepan. Scrape the seeds from the vanilla bean into the cream along with the pod. Add the peppercorns and ½ cup of the sugar and place over medium heat. When it comes to a simmer, with small bubbles around the edges, move to a cooler part of the grill to steep for at least 5 minutes.
2. Meanwhile, "bloom" the gelatin sheets in a bowl of ice water for 2 minutes until softened. Lift the sheets from the water and squeeze gently to remove excess water. Add the gelatin to the infused cream and whisk to combine. Strain through a fine-mesh sieve or cheesecloth and divide among 4 large (6- to 8-ounce / 170- to 227-g) ramekins. Cover with plastic wrap and refrigerate until set, at least 2 hours and up to 24 hours.
3. Preheat griddle to medium-high heat and brush with olive oil.
4. Toss the plums in honey, oil, and a pinch of salt and cook over medium heat until nicely charred, about 90 seconds per side. Using tongs, remove the plums and let cool. Slice the plums and place into a saucepan over medium heat with the remaining ½ cup sugar and the water. Cook until the liquid is syrupy, about 10 minutes. Let cool and then serve atop the cold panna cotta.

Avocado Pizza Bites with Bacon

Prep time: 5 minutes | Cook time: 10 minutes | Serves 4 to 6

2 small avocados
1 tablespoon lime juice
½ teaspoon garlic salt
½ teaspoon onion powder

Dash of hot sauce
1 (13.8-ounce / 391-g) can pizza dough
4 strips bacon, diced
3 tablespoons olive oil
½ cup corn kernels

1. Remove the pits and stems from the avocados and scrape the flesh from the skins with a spoon. Mash the avocado in a medium bowl with the lime juice, garlic salt, onion powder, and hot sauce. You can make this up to a day ahead, but when the avocado is exposed to air it will quickly discolor, so refrigerate with plastic wrap directly on the avocado to prevent it from discoloring.
2. Bring the griddle grill to medium-high heat. Roll out the pizza dough and cut into about 12 squares, or use a round cookie cutter to cut into 12 disks.
3. On one side of the grill, begin cooking the diced bacon. On the other side, pour about 3 tablespoons of olive oil, and spread it into a very thin layer with a spatula or paper towel. Place the pizza dough on the griddle in the oil and cook the dough for about 90 seconds. Flip, and while the second side of the pizza is cooking, add the corn to the bacon and allow it to cook in the bacon grease.
4. Flip the pizza dough frequently, about every 60 seconds, until it turns golden brown and the dough has cooked through, for a total of 6 minutes.
5. When the bacon is crisp but not burned, about 6 minutes, the corn should also have some color from being cooked on the griddle grill. Scoop the bacon and corn salsa onto a paper towel, allowing the bacon fat to absorb.
6. To assemble, schmear about a tablespoon of the avocado mixture onto the grilled pizza dough and top with a teaspoon of the corn and bacon salsa.

Chocolate Butter Mousse

Prep time: 3 minutes | Cook time: 5 minutes | Serves 4

8 ounces (227 g) dark chocolate (70% cacao), coarsely chopped
1 cup heavy cream
3 eggs, separated
1 teaspoon salt, plus more for the egg whites
¾ cup sugar
½ cup (1 stick) butter
1 teaspoon ground cinnamon
1 teaspoon ground instant espresso
1 teaspoon ground chipotle or smoked paprika
1 teaspoon vanilla extract

1. To smoke the chocolate, place it in a small heatproof bowl. Put the bowl in a smoker (the smoker temperature should be very low, under 80ºF (27ºC). Using a hand mixer on high speed, whisk the heavy cream until soft peaks form. Place the bowl over ice to keep cold. Rinse and dry the beaters.
2. In a separate bowl, combine the egg whites and a pinch of salt and mix on high speed for about 30 seconds. While the mixer is running, slowly add ½ cup of the sugar and mix until glossy, stiff peaks have formed. Set aside in a cool place. Rinse and dry the beaters again.
3. In a large bowl, combine the egg yolks, the remaining ¼ cup sugar, the cinnamon, espresso, chipotle, vanilla, and the 1 teaspoon salt. Mix on high speed until doubled in volume, about 3 minutes.
4. Preheat griddle to medium heat. Combine the chocolate and butter in the top of a double boiler and place on the griddle to melt over medium heat. Immediately stir in the egg yolk mixture until no streaks remain. Carefully fold in the egg white mixture, working in two batches, and then add the whipped cream in two batches, trying not to deflate the mixture too much. Divide the mousse among 4 large (6- to 8-ounce / 170- to 227-g) ramekins and refrigerate until set, at least 1 hour and up to 24 hours. Serve chilled.

Banana Trifle with Peanut Streusel

Prep time: 5 minutes | Cook time: 12 minutes | Serves 4

For the Toasted Peanut Streusel:

1 cup (2 sticks) butter
1 cup all-purpose flour
½ cup granulated sugar
½ cup chopped salted peanuts
1 teaspoon ground cinnamon
1 teaspoon salt
1½ cups Mascarpone
½ cup smooth peanut butter
3 tablespoons confectioners' sugar
2 tablespoons honey, plus more for coating
Whole milk, as needed
4 bananas
Oil, for coating

1. To make the streusel: Melt the butter in griddle over medium heat. Add the flour, granulated sugar, peanuts, cinnamon, and salt, and stir continuously until everything is toasted but not burnt, about 10 minutes. Set aside to cool.
2. In a bowl, whisk together the mascarpone, peanut butter, confectioners' sugar, honey, and just enough milk to give it the consistency of thick whipped cream.
3. Preheat griddle to medium-high heat and brush with olive oil.
4. Peel the bananas, slice each in half lengthwise, and toss with oil and honey to coat. Cook over medium heat until caramelized, about 2 minutes per side. Transfer to a plate or cutting board and cut each banana half into four pieces.
5. In a clear-sided trifle dish or in individual ramekins or jelly jars, layer the mascarpone mixture, the bananas, and the streusel; repeat so you end up with 6 layers total. Serve immediately.

Popcorn with Butter

Prep time: 4 minutes | Cook time: 4 minutes | Serves 2 to 4

3 tablespoons peanut oil
½ cup popcorn kernels
3 tablespoons butter
Salt, to taste

1. Prepare your griddle for two-zone cooking.
2. Bring the griddle grill to medium-high heat and add the peanut oil. While it is heating, place 5 popcorn kernels in the oil. When 2 or 3 pop, add the butter to the oil and pour in the remaining kernels. Cover immediately with a tall pan or spaghetti pot.
3. When the popcorn starts popping, you will need to stir it in the oil to get all the kernels to pop and prevent the popped corn from burning. Using insulated gloves, potholders, or thick kitchen towels, agitate the popcorn by moving the pan or pot from side to side on the griddle without lifting. Cook for about 4 minutes, or until the popping slows down to once every few seconds.
4. When all the corn is popped, slide the pot or pan and popcorn to the cool side of the grill and remove the lid. Use two spatulas to scoop up the hot popcorn and transfer to a bowl. Serve with salt and additional seasonings as desired.

Honey Fruit with Yogurt

Prep time: 3 minutes | Cook time: 2 minutes | Serves 4

2 pounds (907 g) fruit, such as pineapples, melons, star fruits, plantains, mangos, apricot, figs, peaches, apples, or pears, peeled, seeded, or cored if necessary
Oil, for coating
¼ cup honey, for grilling, plus more for serving
1 cup plain Greek-style yogurt, for serving

1. Preheat griddle to medium-high heat and brush with olive oil..
2. Cut the fruit into large pieces about 1 inch thick. Toss with the oil to coat. Place each piece over the griddle and cook for about 2 minutes. Using tongs, rotate the fruit 90ºF (32ºC) and continue cooking for another minute. Flip and repeat on the other side. You're not looking to "cook" the fruit so much as heat it through and give it nice grill marks. Brush the fruit lightly with the ¼ cup honey while grilling. Transfer to a serving platter or individual dishes and serve warm with a dollop of yogurt drizzled with honey.

Chapter 9 Sauces

Vinegar Honey Sauce

Prep time: 5 minutes | Cook time: 0 minutes | Makes 2 cups

1¼ cups balsamic vinegar
½ cup water
¼ cup honey
¼ cup cooking oil
1 tablespoon Italian seasoning
1 teaspoon salt
1 teaspoon white pepper

1. Put ingredients in a medium bowl and whisk until combined. Use immediately or store refrigerated for up to 10 days.

Mirin and Soy Sauce

Prep time: 4 minutes | Cook time: 0 minutes | Makes 2 cups

¾ cup water
½ cup mirin
½ cup soy sauce
¼ cup sesame oil
1 tablespoon garlic
powder
1 tablespoon ground ginger
1 tablespoon grated fresh ginger

1. Put ingredients in a medium bowl and whisk until combined. Use immediately or store refrigerated for up to 10 days.

Lemon and Thyme Sauce

Prep time: 4 minutes | Cook time: 0 minutes | Makes 2 cups

1 cup low-sodium chicken broth
½ cup freshly squeezed lemon juice
¼ cup cooking oil
¼ cup water
1 tablespoon finely minced fresh chives
1 tablespoon fresh thyme
1 tablespoon finely minced garlic

1. Put ingredients in a medium bowl and whisk until combined. Use immediately or store refrigerated for up to 10 days.

White Wine Sherry Sauce

Prep time: 4 minutes | Cook time: 0 minutes | Makes 2 cups

1 cup dry white wine
½ cup water
¼ cup cooking sherry
¼ cup cooking oil
2 tablespoons finely minced shallots
1 tablespoon dried
parsley
1 tablespoon finely minced garlic
1 tablespoon finely minced capers
1 teaspoon salt
1 teaspoon pepper

1. Put ingredients in a medium bowl and whisk until combined. Use immediately or store refrigerated for up to 10 days.

Ketchup Juice Sauce

Prep time: 4 minutes | Cook time: 0 minutes | Makes 2 cups

1 cup ketchup
⅓ cup cider vinegar
⅓ cup apple juice
¼ cup Worcestershire sauce
¼ cup sriracha
2 tablespoons water
2 tablespoons onion
powder
2 tablespoons garlic powder
2 tablespoons sugar
2 tablespoons brown sugar
2 tablespoons tomato paste

1. Put ingredients in a medium bowl and whisk until combined. Use immediately or store refrigerated for up to 10 days.

Lemony Rosemary and Gin Sour

Prep time: 5 minutes | Cook time: 0 minutes | Serves 4

8 sprigs of rosemary
Ice cubes
¾ cup gin
6 tablespoons freshly squeezed lemon juice

(from 2 lemons)
¼ cup simple syrup
Lemon slices, plain or grilled, for garnish (optional)

1. Preheat griddle to medium-high heat and brush with oil.
2. Burn the rosemary on the griddle by holding it with tongs over high heat until the leaves start to smoke. Place 1 sprig in each of 4 rocks glasses filled with ice and put the remaining sprigs in a cocktail shaker. Add the gin, lemon juice, and simple syrup to the shaker with ice. Shake well and strain into the glasses. Garnish with lemon slices, if desired.

Thyme and Lemon Cocktail

Prep time: 6 minutes | Cook time: 0 minutes | Serves 8

8 lemons, halved
16 sprigs of thyme
Ice cubes

4 cups ice water
1½ cups vodka
½ cup agave or simple syrup

1. Preheat griddle to medium-high heat and brush with olive oil.
2. Place the lemons, cut side down, over high heat until they are charred and soft, about 3 minutes. While the lemons char, using tongs, hold 8 of the thyme sprigs over high heat just until they start to color and give off wisps of smoke.
3. Add the remaining 8 thyme sprigs to a cocktail shaker, squeeze in the lemon juice, and add a couple ice cubes. Shake very well and strain into a pitcher. Add the ice water, vodka, and agave, and stir until the agave is dissolved.
4. Serve the drinks in ice-filled glasses garnished with a charred thyme sprig.

Tomato Vodka

Prep time: 10 minutes | Cook time: 0 minutes | Serves 4

3 plum tomatoes, about 10 ounces (283 g) total
½ habanero chile, stemmed and seeded (use gloves or a paper towel when handling habaneros)
½ garlic clove
1 tablespoon fresh or store-bought horserad-

ish
1 tablespoon Worcestershire sauce
1 tablespoon freshly squeezed lemon juice
6 ounces (170 g) vodka
Celery sticks, lemon wedges, and/or pickled peperoncini, for garnish

1. Preheat griddle to medium-high heat and brush with oil.
2. Cook the tomatoes over medium heat, turning occasionally, until lightly charred and soft all over, about 10 minutes. Meanwhile, using tongs, hold the habanero over medium heat until it starts to brown and soften, about 2 minutes. Transfer the tomatoes and habanero to a blender together with the garlic, horseradish, Worcestershire, and lemon juice. Blend until very smooth, then strain through a fine-mesh strainer or cheesecloth into a pitcher, discarding any tomato skins that remain. Stir in the vodka and divide among ice-filled glasses, garnishing as desired.

Orange and Bourbon Cocktail

Prep time: 6 minutes | Cook time: 0 minutes | Serves 4

4 blood oranges
¾ cup bourbon

1 tablespoon sugar, plus more for rimming the glasses

1. Preheat griddle to medium-high heat and brush with olive oil.
2. Cut 3 of the oranges in half and grill, cut side down, over high heat until charred. Halve the remaining orange, cut into thick slices, and grill until charred on both sides; set aside. Squeeze the orange halves to get 1 cup juice.
3. Add the juice, bourbon, and sugar to a cocktail shaker. Add ice to fill the shaker almost to the rim. Shake well for about 30 seconds to ensure the sugar dissolves and the drink is well chilled. Strain into sugar-rimmed coupe or martini glasses and garnish each with a charred orange slice.

Margarita with Lime

Prep time: 6 minutes | Cook time: 0 minutes | Serves 4

5 limes, halved
Honey, for coating
Salt and ground chipotle chile, to taste

1 cup tequila
½ cup Cointreau

1. Preheat griddle to medium heat and brush with olive oil.
2. Coat the cut side of the limes with honey and place, cut side down, over medium heat until charred and soft, about 4 minutes. Remove from heat and, when they are cool enough to handle, squeeze the lime halves to get ½ cup juice.
3. Mix salt and chipotle in a 2:1 ratio. Moisten rims of 4 glasses with the squeezed lime halves and dip into the chipotle salt. Fill glasses with ice.
4. Add the lime juice to a cocktail shaker with the tequila, Cointreau, and a couple ice cubes. Shake very well and strain into prepared glasses.

Appendix 1: Measurement Conversion Chart

VOLUME EQUIVALENTS(DRY)

US STANDARD	METRIC (APPROXIMATE)
1/8 teaspoon	0.5 mL
1/4 teaspoon	1 mL
1/2 teaspoon	2 mL
3/4 teaspoon	4 mL
1 teaspoon	5 mL
1 tablespoon	15 mL
1/4 cup	59 mL
1/2 cup	118 mL
3/4 cup	177 mL
1 cup	235 mL
2 cups	475 mL
3 cups	700 mL
4 cups	1 L

VOLUME EQUIVALENTS(LIQUID)

US STANDARD	US STANDARD (OUNCES)	METRIC (APPROXIMATE)
2 tablespoons	1 fl.oz.	30 mL
1/4 cup	2 fl.oz.	60 mL
1/2 cup	4 fl.oz.	120 mL
1 cup	8 fl.oz.	240 mL
1 1/2 cup	12 fl.oz.	355 mL
2 cups or 1 pint	16 fl.oz.	475 mL
4 cups or 1 quart	32 fl.oz.	1 L
1 gallon	128 fl.oz.	4 L

TEMPERATURES EQUIVALENTS

FAHRENHEIT(F)	CELSIUS(C) (APPROXIMATE)
225 °F	107 °C
250 °F	120 °C
275 °F	135 °C
300 °F	150 °C
325 °F	160 °C
350 °F	180 °C
375 °F	190 °C
400 °F	205 °C
425 °F	220 °C
450 °F	235 °C
475 °F	245 °C
500 °F	260 °C

WEIGHT EQUIVALENTS

US STANDARD	METRIC (APPROXIMATE)
1 ounce	28 g
2 ounces	57 g
5 ounces	142 g
10 ounces	284 g
15 ounces	425 g
16 ounces (1 pound)	455 g
1.5 pounds	680 g
2 pounds	907 g

Appendix 2: Recipe Index